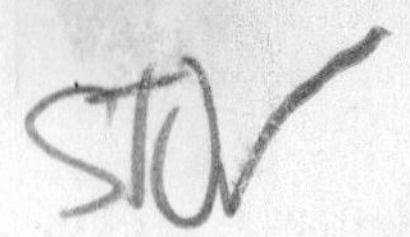

D0007795

OUT ON A LIMB

OUT ON A LIMB

by

LOUISE BAKER

Author of

"PARTY LINE"

WHITTLESEY HOUSE

MC GRAW-HILL BOOK COMPANY, INC.

New York : London

OUT ON A LIMB

PUBLISHED BY WHITTLESEY HOUSE
A Division of the McGraw-Hill Book Company, Inc.

Printed in the United States of America

CONTENTS

OUT ON A LIMB

CHAPTER I

Honeymoon with a Handicap

I BECAME a minor celebrity in my home town at the precocious age of eight. This distinction was not bestowed on me because I was a bright little trick like Joel Kupperman, nor because I could play the piano like a velvet-pantalooned prodigy. I was, to keep the record straight, a decidedly normal and thoroughly untalented child. I wasn't even pretty. My paternal grandmother, in fact, often pointed out that I was the plainest girl in three generations of our family, and she had a photograph album full of tintypes to prove it. She hoped that I'd at least be good, but I didn't achieve my fame because of my virtue either. My memorable record in the annals of the town was the result of mere accident.

Completely against parental advice, I took an unauthorized spin on a neighbor boy's bicycle. It was a shiny, red vehicle that I admired inordinately but thoroughly misunderstood. I couldn't even reach the pedals. However, I started a perilous descent of a hill, yelling with giddy excitement. At the bottom, I swung around a corner where I entangled myself and bicycle with an oncoming automobile. As part, apparently, of an ordained pattern, the car was piloted by a woman who was just learning to drive. Her ignorance and mine combined to victimize me.

A crowd gathered. Strong arms lifted me. I had a momentary horrified clarity during which I screamed "Mama!" as I got what proved to be a farewell glimpse of my right leg.

When I regained consciousness ten days later in a white hospital bed, with the blankets propped over me like a canopy, I had one foot in the grave. It was a heavy penalty to pay for my pirated first and last ride on a bicycle.

However, I was famous. My name, which in the past had excited no stirring sentiments, was mentioned with eulogy in ten county newspapers; five doctors had hovered over me in consultation; twelve churches and one synagogue had offered up prayers for my recovery; and I had been in surgery three times.

The last trip was the fateful one. My old friend Dr. Craig, who had never administered anything more serious than pink pills to me during my brief and healthy span, in final desperation for my life, amputated my right leg above the knee. He then, if there is any truth in local lore, went into his office and had himself a good cry over the whole business.

There were many tears shed over me in the name

of my youth. I was, it was mournfully agreed, too young to have such a life-shattering tragedy strike me. Since no one has wept over me in a long time, it is nice to recollect that I once provoked a lot of strong emotion.

However, the emotion bolstered a false theory—the theory that I was too young. I was, I am convinced, precisely the right age. I am not one of those cheerfully smiling brave-hearts who claims to be just too-too happy about a handicap and grateful for the spiritual strength that bearing my burden has bestowed on me. Spiritual strength bores me—you can't dance on it, and I'm certain it never receives the wholehearted admiration accorded a well-shaped gam. I'd much rather have two legs, even though a pair of nylon stockings lasts twice as long when you're a uniped. But, granted that Fate has cast an evil designing eye on an appendage, let her make the graceful gesture and snip while the victim is young!

I understand that it was a tossup for a while whether my family would have to invest in a tombstone or a pair of crutches for me. But ten weeks of concentrated medical attention combined with my normal healthy resiliency, and I was issued to the world again as damaged goods. Even then, I think I suspected what I *know* now. Fate, for all her worst intentions, was foiled in some fantastic way. She had her pound of flesh, to be sure, but she left me primed for a unique adventure in living that I should never have experienced with the orthodox number of legs.

Perhaps I realized the new turn life had taken when my sister sat by my bedside and sobbed out an ill-made promise that I would never have to help her with the dishes again so long as I lived. Instead of shoving an affidavit at her, I was feeling just sick enough to fancy myself Elsie Dinsmore or her first cousin, Pollyanna. I lightheadedly assured her I'd be back at the pan as soon as I got some crutches. Within a few months we were striking blows at each other over that regrettable exchange of sisterly sentiments.

If I had been a little sharper-witted and had possessed a more pliable pair of parents, I believe I might very well have developed into the most thoroughly spoiled brat the world has ever seen. As it was, I made a close approximation to that pinnacle before I fell under the weight of my own accomplishment.

Even before I left the hospital my sudden power over people was showing itself. First of all, with completely unconscious brilliance, I chose rather inspired subjects to discuss during my five days of post-operative delirium. I rambled on feverishly but with moving feeling about a large doll with real golden hair and blue eyes that opened and closed. I even conveniently mentioned the awesome price and just where such a doll might be purchased, and I sighed over my father's attested poverty which prevented him from buying me this coveted treasure. My delirious words were passed on promptly. The head nurse quoted my pathetic plea to our local telephone operator. The news spread. "That poor little crippled child in the hospital, a breath away from death, wants a doll. . . ."

Our local toy merchant was no fool. He let ten customers buy identical yellow-haired dolls at $7.98 apiece, even though he knew well enough for what child they were all destined. He also sold seven dark-haired, porcelain-faced beauties when he ran out of blondes. And he did a regular Christmas-bulk business in doll beds, parcheesi games, paper dolls, puzzles, paintboxes and books. People averted their eyes, I understand, when they passed the Super Ball-bearing Flyer roller skates that I had also mentioned during my providential spell of wistful delirium. The sight of the roller skates brought a tear to many an eye and usually raised the ante assigned for a present to me by at least a dollar. The merchant decided it might help business to put bicycles in his window.

When I left the hospital it took two cars to transport my loot. I was as well equipped with toys as a princess. Everybody in town, including owners of flower beds on which I had trod and windows which I had broken, suddenly loved me and came bearing gifts. It was a warmhearted, friendly little town. Although it claimed no psychologists or occupational therapists, it was, I believe, the ideal environment for the normal adjustment of a handicapped child.

By putting different colored ribbons on the ten blonde dolls, I was able to tell them apart and I named them Alice, Virginia, Araminta Ann, Elizabeth, Caroline, Janet, Shirley, Phronsey (after a member of a distinguished fictional family named Pepper), Gwendolyn, and Hortense—a hateful name, but I poked Hortense's eye out so she didn't deserve anything better. It didn't occur to me to share the dolls with my less lavishly endowed friends. I merely displayed them smugly and let my playmates swallow the water in their mouths.

It took me just ten weeks in the hospital to acquire seventeen new dolls and a very selfish disposition. In time, of course, my parents made me give away the dolls—all except Hortense whose handicap eventually appealed to my better nature, and Araminta Ann who was, for some reason, my favorite. As for my selfishness, that was spanked out of me when my parents finally came to the conclusion that they were going to have to live with me for a long, long time, and the prospect was anything but cheering.

The first spanking was the hardest—on Father. Later they were much harder on me and easier on him. I'll never forget the shock of that first, firm-handed discipline.

I arrived at the sly conclusion very soon after I

came home from the hospital that I didn't really have to be delirious to get what I wanted. Three months before, I was a reasonably well-mannered child who even hesitated to hint for cookies when visiting my own grandmother. Now I was a precocious little gold-digger, and anyone was my fair game. I possessed a magic lamp, a wishing ring—or something just as efficient and much more realistic. I could sit in my wheel chair and watch the normal children playing outdoors. All I had to mumble by way of magic words was, "I'll never be able to run again, will I?" This sad little speech—rhetorically speaking—flung everyone within hearing flat on their faces in abject servitude. The moment was ripe to make almost any demand. As a cousin of mine in reminiscing about our youth once said, "You sure were a little stinker!"

On the particular occasion which was to prove a prologue to the inevitable ripping off of the velvet glove, we had a caller. It was Mrs. Royce, an old friend of the family. She made a great emotional flutter over me. She sniffled into her handkerchief and claimed to have a cold, but she didn't fool me—not for a minute!

"And what shall I bring to this little girlie next time I come?" she cooed at me between her attacks of pseudo-sinusitus.

"Well—" I pondered carefully and commercially. "I can't run or anything any more, you know. I can only sit on the floor and play all by myself." Long sigh. Pause. "I think I'd like to have you bring me an electric train."

I knew well enough the financial magnitude of my aspiration. Electric trains had been discussed frequently in our household. I had about as much chance of getting an electric train from Father as I had of getting fifty-one per cent of the preferred stock in the Atchison, Topeka, and Santa Fe. However, I could see that my speech had worked new havoc on Mrs. Royce's cold, and I was confidently expectant. But although I didn't know it, I had at long last taken the fatal step back to normalcy.

Father cleared his throat noisily and said, "Louise isn't going to have an electric train."

"Oh, now—really!" Kind Mrs. Royce was a childless widow with a solid bank account. "I'd love to give the poor little girlie an electric train."

"No," repeated my father, warming to a role that had once been very familiar to him. "We don't want her to have an electric train."

"You see," Mother brought up reinforcements. Obviously, in her own mysterious manner, she was reading Father's mind. "We think electric toys are dangerous. She might get a shock."

"Oh, yes—a shock. She might at that," Mrs. Royce agreed reluctantly. "I'll think of something just as nice and more suitable for a little girlie." (The next day she presented me with a satin-lined sewing basket equipped with colored thread, blunt scissors, and a red strawberry in which to embed needles. A splendid thing, that basket, but alas, I wasn't that kind of a girlie.)

Farewells were said and Mrs. Royce departed, after patting my cheek.

"I won't *either* get a shock!" I cried, as soon as the door closed.

"Not from an electric train, you won't!" said Father, and there was a regretful but determined look in his eye. "But you're due for a shock right now."

He headed straight for me. He lifted me gently out of my wheel chair and carefully tilted me over his knee. I saw the tortured expression on Mother's face and heard her gasp. But she didn't make a move to rescue me, even when I screamed, "*Mama!* I'm crippled!" with all the wicked chicanery of my little black heart.

Father spanked me. The honeymoon with my handicap was over.

CHAPTER II

On Foot Again

I OCCUPIED a wheel chair much longer than was actually necessary merely because there were no crutches readily available in my size. Although the local drugstore carried a few rental crutches to accommodate the temporarily disabled, it was apparently assumed that no one as small as I would ever be clumsy enough to need props. Mr. Bennett, the pharmacist, stopped by one evening to measure me, and he sent off an order to a San Francisco orthopedic supply house. It happened that the California distributor was also temporarily out of my size. So my first pair of crutches came all the way across the continent from a crutch manufacturer in Newark, New Jersey.

Waiting for the crutches to arrive was a slow and tantalizing ordeal. I looked up Newark on a map and it seemed more remote than the North Pole. I felt I might get better results by writing to Santa Claus.

I was certainly ready to walk! My strength was definitely back. In fact, it was as gusty and explosive as a hurricane bottled up in a barrel. Dolls went dull on me. I had read all the children's books in the public library and I knew my own books by heart. I was headed through the *Encyclopaedia Britannica* on the theory that I would learn a few facts every day until I knew absolutely everything, but the going got grim before I'd made a dent in the *A*'s. I was sick of playing jacks on the front porch. I was even bored with mumblety-peg, the most vigorous and hardy sedentary game I knew. The only recreation I could tolerate was plowing up the front lawn while rolling my wheel chair over it in a self-invented polo-croquet. To play this game I required two or three competitors—also mounted on vehicles of their choice. The lawn was beginning to look somewhat haggard, and so was Mother. I was already a veteran hopper. I bounced all over the house, much to the concern of my grandmother, who was convinced I'd disarrange all my internal organs.

"And then where will you be, young lady?" she popped the moot question. "No leg—and queer things wrong with your insides, too." Grandmother's complete lack of tact was undoubtedly good, rugged training for me. Certainly after Grandmother, no one was ever able to embarrass me.

Every afternoon my sister Bernice pushed me to the corner where we had a clear, three-block view of Father's direct route home from the office. Usually several of the neighborhood children kept the vigil with us.

Finally, one day when hope was almost dead, we spotted Father looking very jaunty. When he saw us, he waved and held up a brown paper-wrapped parcel. Then he abandoned all dignity and sprinted down the street.

"They've come!" I shouted. "The crutches from Newark, New Jersey!" Johnny Nesbitt, who lived next door to us, took up the tidings and ran with them up and down both sides of our block. Children spewed out of houses. By the time we got home, a large audience had accumulated. You'd have thought I was about to uncrate a Shetland pony.

I probably never in my life unwrapped a more significant package than the one that contained that first pair of yellow pine crutches. One dollar and twenty-five cents' worth—Mr. Bennett let us have them wholesale.

They must have been very small crutches, but they seemed frightfully heavy and cumbersome as I freed them from the paper and twine. Eagerly I slid out of my wheel chair.

"Maybe you'd better wait until later to try them," Mother suggested nervously.

"*Wait!*" I gasped. What had I been doing for the past interminable month! Then I saw the fear on Mother's face. She thought I'd fall. It was obvious my silently pitying audience shared her dire expectation. Suddenly, so did I.

"Of course, she won't wait!" Father announced sensibly. He slipped one crutch under each of my arms. He knew I was a show-off and would try harder in front of my friends. I grasped the handles.

"Now lift the crutches ahead of you," he instructed me. "You've seen people walk on crutches–remember when Jim Ralston broke his ankle. Just swing your foot up in front of them. That's all there is to it."

My knee shook, but I walked alone across the room. I was incredibly clumsy, but I was once more self-propelling and I felt triumphant.

My father, I think, recognized from the start that other people's fears and pity would always be more threatening to my security than my own. He worked hard at concealing his personal concern over me and he was singularly successful. So successful that some of our neighbors regarded him as unfeeling. So successful that he even gave me the comforting impression that he thought children with two legs were just a little bit odd.

"It's easy," I said breathlessly. "Very easy." I started to sit down on the davenport and made my first technical discovery. Crutches won't bend. They must be put aside before you start to fold up. Father rescued me as I tipped over backward.

"I sure bet it's fun to walk on crutches," Johnny Nesbitt sighed enviously.

"Oh, it certainly is!" I crossed my fingers to protect myself from the bold-faced lie. Actually, I spoke the truth; walking on crutches is great fun, as I discovered eventually.

"Could I try them just for a second?" Johnny asked.

"Me, too!" It was a chorus.

Crutches are invariably fascinating to children. It surprised Mother, I am sure, that they were immediately treated like a new velocipede or a scooter. Everyone lined up and took turns for the remainder of the afternoon. The children in my immediate neighborhood and most of my classmates in school all became quite adept at walking on crutches.

For Johnny Nesbitt, at least, the skill proved useful. Last year he wrote me from an army hospital where he was convalescing from a leg wound received in the Pacific war theater. "The eyes nearly popped out of the nurse's head when I put the crutches under my arms for the first time, whinnied at her, and then did the five-gaited horse act down the hospital corridor." The five gaits were a spectacular and horsey bit of fancy work that I invented early in my career on crutches.

Lending the crutches, it is true, became something of a burden. A person dependent on crutches likes to have them in sight every minute, and preferably in hand. I have no more menacing, though innocent, enemy than the restaurant waiter who politely snatches my sticks as he seats me at a table and rushes off with them to a check room or some other mysterious place of concealment. It gives me the frantic feeling a normal person might experience if some fiend padlocked his feet together and then, with a hollow chortle, tossed the key out the window.

A rule was eventually laid down in the neighborhood that a child might, with permission, borrow the crutches providing they didn't go beyond the range of my vision. The crutches were my only possessions with which I was allowed, and even encouraged, to be selfish. As Father pointed out, "After all, you don't go around borrowing other people's legs. It amounts to the same thing."

The only share-the-crutch plan that was completely successful was the one worked out by Barbara Bradley and me. Barbara and I were best friends, but we were prevented by my crutches from walking to school side by side, holding hands, or arms entwined. Our scheme solved this problem. Barbara put a crutch under her left arm and I put one under my right. By resting our free arms on each other's shoulders, we supported each other in the middle. By this complicated arrangement, we walked to school every day, and resembled, for all the world, a badly damaged pair of Siamese twins.

Grandmother telephoned the night the crutches arrived. "I hear the crutches have come." She sighed deeply and with apparent regret. Grandma was a cynic. "I expect you'll be tramping around the neighborhood into all kinds of trouble again. Now, listen to me, you probably think you know it all—about handling your crutches—but let me remind you that there are plenty of older and wiser heads than yours." Grandma was argumentative, even in monologue.

"I can walk just fine, Grandma," I bragged.

"That's what *you* say," Grandmother sniffed. "You are to go over and see Mrs. Ferris tomorrow, and she'll teach you how to walk like a lady, if you've got sense enough to pay attention."

Mrs. Ferris was eighty-three and had been bedridden for seven years, ever since she came to town to live with her daughter. It seemed beyond possibility that the withered, little wisp could teach me anything, least of all, how to walk.

But Grandmother and I had an agreement. I minded her implicitly, in the expectation of deferred reward. When I got to heaven—a possibility that Grandma didn't wholeheartedly anticipate—she would, of course, already be there and she promised to put in a good word for me. Grandma and God were on excellent terms although, regrettably, the same couldn't be said of Grandma and anyone else. I sometimes vaguely wondered what *God* saw in Grandma.

"All right, Grandma," I agreed, "I will go over and ask Mrs. Ferris how to walk." It wouldn't have been good form to demand what Mrs. Ferris knew about the business.

As a matter of fact, Mrs. Ferris knew a great deal. She had been injured in an accident and for fifteen years of her active life, she had walked on crutches.

I don't have a Phi Beta key; Mr. Powers never cast a covetous eye in my direction; and I can't do parlor tricks; but I do allow myself one immodest, extravagant vanity. It is the conviction that no one in the world can handle a pair of crutches better than I. I have my own bag of tricks collected during twenty-eight years of experience. It was a little old lady, ten times my age, who really planted my foot and my crutches firmly on the ground and started me on the quest for a wing for my heel.

Mrs. Ferris's advice was practical and sound, and included the basic technique that distinguishes an experienced lifer on crutches from the temporary time-server.

"First of all," Mrs. Ferris instructed me, "do *not* lean on your armpits and do *not* swing your whole body when you take a step. Experts can walk easily with no saddletops at all on their crutches. Lean all your weight on the palms of your hands. The only time when it is necessary to bear weight on the tops of your crutches is when you are carrying something in your hands."

Not only is it much more graceful and comfortable to "walk on your hands," but it is protection against injury of the brachial nerves, particularly vulnerable in the armpits. Injury to these nerves, with the resultant so-called "crutch paralysis," is the blackest specter that haunts a permanent crutch-user.

Mrs. Ferris and I spent an hour together every day for several weeks. I strutted up and down her bedroom while she criticized my technique. My most persistent error was spreading the crutches out to form a wide tripod and swinging my whole body with each stride instead of stepping out with my foot in a normal walking motion.

"Hold them close to your sides! Make them look as if they grew there!" Mrs. Ferris repeated over and over. "Keep your body perpendicular! Walk with your foot, not with your torso."

Mrs. Ferris's methods were not only practical but aesthetic. Making the crutches as nearly anatomical as possible, crowding them to my sides, also prevented me from planting a booby trap with them. Flung out, one on each side, in the instinctive stance of a beginner, they created an infernal device for tripping up unwary pedestrians. Not that I haven't, with design, upset a few minor enemies in my time. This trick is a mild version of the perfect crime. The victim always assumes that he was in the wrong and, even sprawled out on the sidewalk, apologizes.

Before Mrs. Ferris graduated me from her kindergarten, she had me walking with a full cup of water in my hand and two books on my head.

"When you can recite your multiplication tables as you walk down the street, without once thinking about your crutches, you have really succeeded," Mrs. Ferris told me.

I didn't know my multiplication tables, but I took her literally and started studying them. By the time I'd mastered my eights, I'd practically quit walking in favor of running, and so I never did learn my nines.

CHAPTER III

Best Foot Forward

GRANDMA said it was an outrage. "One of two terrible things will happen," she predicted. "She'll either kill herself, or worse yet, she'll get along fine and end up in vaudeville. We've had six clergymen, a smattering of lawyers and doctors and a raft of school teachers and good honest farmers in this family. We've never had a show girl!"

"What about Great-great-great-cousin Thaddeus?" Bernice demanded, just to keep things interesting.

"Hah! That was on your mother's side." Grandmother nodded her head with satisfaction. "And even that rascal wasn't a show girl."

"But he was a perfectly marvelous outlaw and shot a man in cold blood," I bragged. "That's just as bad."

"It's not just as bad," Grandma stated with finality.

"Now, listen to me, Mother." On rare occasions Father was bold enough to stand up to Grandma. "We're off the subject. Louise is nine years old and she wants some roller skates for her birthday. Is there anything so strange in that? Bernice had roller skates when she was nine."

"That's different. Bernice didn't make an unnatural spectacle of herself using them. Everyone will stare, and first thing you know, Louise will become a disgusting little exhibitionist and skate off with a carnival or something and you'll never see her again. It's a pity she isn't a little lady, content to learn to sew and do water colors and read good literature. I never skated when I was her age, and I had both my limbs."

When Grandmother spoke of her own legs, she called them limbs, as if they were slightly more refined than ordinary appendages.

In reality Grandmother wasn't the sharp-bladed battle-ax she pretended. She was really fond of me and every new hurdle I wanted to leap seemed twice as hazardous to her as the last one.

But Father bought me the skates. I had already experimented with Barbara Bradley's and knew I could manage. With a skate on my one foot and a crutch on each side, I propelled myself. My balance was exceptional—as is most every uniped's. This is a natural physical compensation that develops quickly—as do strong shoulders and arms. After a few good shoves, I could lift up my crutches and coast along easily on the one skate, pushing with my sticks only when I needed fresh momentum. For a child of nine, supposedly sentenced to a plodding pedestrianism, getting back on wheels was sheer ecstasy.

Of course, I fell frequently while developing skill

on roller skates. Every child sprawls when learning to skate. I am not convinced that I spread myself out on the sidewalk any more often than a normal child does. But this is the curious fact: my playmates, wise in their childhood, accepted my spills as inevitable to the process of learning—but adults didn't. No army of rescuers advanced double-quick time to pick up any other youngster on the block when he came a cropper. But whenever I took a header, for all the turmoil the minor catastrophe created, it might have been a four-car smashup at a busy intersection. All the women in our neighborhood must have squandered their days with their eyes glued to a crack in the window blind while I learned to roller skate. For a brief time, I was as prominent as a lurid scandal.

Whenever I fell, out swarmed the women in droves, clucking and fretting like a bunch of bereft mother hens. It was kind of them, and in retrospect I appreciate their solicitude, but at the time I resented and was greatly embarrassed by their interference. It set me apart and emphasized my difference. For they assumed that no routine hazard to skating—no stick or stone—upset my flying wheels. It was a foregone conclusion that *I* fell because I was a poor, helpless cripple.

"What must her mother *think!*" was a phrase with which I became very familiar. I know now what my mother thought. Inside our house, she too kept her eye on the crack in the blind, and she wrung her hands and took to biting her fingernails while she developed a lot of fortitude. For Mother differed from the other women in only one particular. She never ran out and picked me up. I believe that Father, a normally devoted husband, threatened homicide if she did.

Eventually, of course, nobody paid any attention to me. The women abandoned their watchful vigils at windows and went back to more pressing problems—their baking and dishwashing. I rolled up and down the street unheeded and was no longer good box office.

However, the roller-skating incident left its mark on me, and consciously or unconsciously, it influenced my future approach to physical activity. I was by nature energetic and athletic. I wanted to engage in all sorts of "inappropriate" games and sports, but I became overly sensitive to failure—foolishly so. I had a stubborn pride that was wounded by any hint that my handicap was a "handicap." It really wasn't much of one, compared to the frustrating handicaps many less fortunate people carry. Still I was practically neurotic over The Word. My feathers ruffled at the drop of it. A wise psychologist friend of mine has since put a name on this attitude of mind. She called it a tendency to overcompensate.

When I learned to swim, I insisted that Father drive me out to the country to a friend's ranch where, in guarded privacy, I went through my dog-paddling period in a muddy irrigation ditch. I forewent the greater comfort and the companionship of the public swimming pool until I not only swam as well as other eleven-year-olds (the age at which I took to the water), but better. Then, when I made a public appearance, no one even noticed my handicap—I falsely deduced.

My swimming ability, in point of fact, probably was more conspicuous than utter ineptitude would have been. But blissfully, I had no such realization. In the water, my arms and shoulders, disciplined into extra strength by my crutches, compensated in the Australian crawl for my one-cylinder flutter kick. I felt completely anonymous—happy moron, me! Actually, I wasn't the least bit anonymous, although my family encouraged me in this wild surmise. My sister tells me that my red bathing cap, bobbing about in the water, was invariably pointed out to bystanders. "See the little girl in the red cap? Would you believe it, she only has one leg!"

The same was true of tennis, which I learned in semisecrecy. Father taught me in the early morning hours when the courts were unpopular. My father didn't permit me to luxuriate in a lot of fancy complexes, but he was sympathetic with my reluctance to display physical clumsiness. Tennis presents more limitations for an amputee than swimming. The basic constraint is the necessity of holding one crutch with just the upper arm, leaving a hand free to manipulate a racket. I heard of a man with a left leg amputation who played tennis with only one crutch. I always used two since I am both right-handed and right-crutched and could not control both a racket and a completely weight-bearing crutch with one arm.

In spite of restrictions, I did fairly well at tennis as a child. I even competed, with average success, in a few junior tournaments. This brief period of minor distinction was not the result of exceptional skill, however. It was rather the happy aftermath of the advantage of earlier and better instruction than my contemporaries. Father was a very able tennis amateur. He was infinitely patient in developing in me a good serve and a strong, deep-court drive to offset my inadequate technique at the net. In playing tennis, I discovered that it is essential to hug the serving line. It is easy to run forward, but not backward, on crutches. I am completely vulnerable at the net or even mid-court where a lob over my head spells defeat. I can't readily retreat to get it on the bounce, and the alternative, a high aerial stroke, invariably makes me drop a crutch.

I enjoy tennis very much, but stacking up all the good points of my game against the poor ones, I come out a mediocre performer. "A good, average housewife tennis player," someone dubbed me—and that is no enviable distinction. I usually compete with people who are better than I, so am rarely victorious—which is perhaps just as well.

Friends who know me, and with whom I play frequently, don't care whether I win or lose. We just play tennis. Some of them avoid cutting and lobs because it keeps our game more rallying, but they are in no way offensively patronizing to me.

Pit a stranger against me, however—especially a male stranger—and he will methodically do one of two things, according to his basic character. He will make the gallant gesture and let me win—which is easily detected and humiliating. Or, he will kill himself before admitting defeat by a one-legged woman.

I once confronted across a net, by the conniving conspiracy of some school friends, a boy who was notoriously cocky on the tennis court. The essence of the cunning plot was that I must defeat this self-advertising fire-eater so ignominiously and completely that he would never again hold up his arrogant head. I had no confidence in my ability to do this and, frankly, neither did my conspiring boy friends. It was such a superb scheme, however, that they were all willing to cooperate on its success. They concluded that if I won, it would be magnificent irony—a baby stealing candy from a man, for a change.

Two boys were assigned to pound away at my

backhand for a week, and spies reported my unsuspecting enemy's weaknesses and strengths. He was definitely not the ball of fire he advertised, but he was better than I, it was mournfully agreed. However, everyone hoped that I could at least give him enough competition to make him feel foolish. I was pledged to outplay myself, even if I folded in complete collapse.

I didn't even know Charlie, the victim, but it all seemed solemnly important to me at the time. I was fifteen, and the prime-mover in the plot was a very handsome muscular gent of seventeen for whose smallest favor I would gladly have given my last leg.

By the most contrived casualness, I was introduced to Charlie at the tennis courts, where he was loudly quoting what Bill Tilden said to him and what smart repartee he handed Bill. The game was arranged. We had decided to contract for only one set, as my well-wishers in their wildest dreams, didn't hope I'd last longer than that.

In analyzing mine and my opponent's weaknesses, one great big one was overlooked. The outcome of that game was not traceable to technique and tenacity and my newly polished backhand, although all these helped, no doubt. The game was won on temper—both mine and Charlie's. To start with, The Cock's first sentence contained fighting words, as far as I was concerned. He said, with a patronizing air, "Sure,

I'll take her on if you guys don't want to bother. I don't mind a bit."

I let this go by unchallenged. I merely seethed. Then he suggested that he should be handicapped if he played me. "I'll give you fifteen," he offered pompously. This was red flag to my bull!

"Pooh! I'll give *you* thirty," I counteroffered. This was red flag to his bull!

We marched out on the court as mad as if we'd just blacked each other's eyes. Temper warms up my reflexes, but it completely melted Charlie's. He belonged to the racket-throwing persuasion.

I must have been dropped on my head as a baby. I can't imagine any other explanation for squandering exertion as extravagantly as I did on that occasion. I wouldn't work that hard today if I were promised the Davis Cup for keeps. Somehow, I got the psychotic notion embedded in my half-a-mind that nothing matter so much as beating Charlie.

As soon as Charlie and I spun for serve, all the tennis games in progress on the other courts stopped immediately, and the players became our spectators. They all belonged in my camp and they helped me by none-too-sporting maneuvers. They worked poor Charlie into impotent fury by catcalls and other impertinences.

When he missed a shot or netted a serve, they'd all yell, "What's s'matter, got a Charlie–*Horse?*" This

was regarded in our high school intellectual circles as overpoweringly witty. Everyone hooted and howled.

"Maybe *you* need some crutches, Charlie!"

"*Fault!*" they'd yell before Charlie's serves even bounced. To ensure a modicum of fair play, I had to call all the shots myself.

In spite of the tremendous nuisance value of my audience and the demoralizing effect on Charlie of his own temper, I had a desperate time beating him. We ran the set, most of the games long deuce-score ordeals, to twelve-ten before I won.

When it was over, my breath was coming in rattling gasps and I looked like a dripping hot beet just out of a stew pot and dragged home by an insensitive cat. Charlie walked off the court and broke up his racket by bashing it against a steel post. He wasn't a very lofty character.

I rode a brief wave of delirious ecstasy while a crowd of what I regarded as exceedingly smooth boys banged me on my aching back and shouted my praises. Then I staggered home to soak my weary heroic bones in a hot tub.

Father peered at me over his paper as I came in and collapsed on the davenport.

"Good *God!*" he gasped. Father was not a swearing man so I must have resembled a sister of Grim Death. "What in a holy name have you been doing?"

"I beat Charlie," I puffed proudly. "Been practicing for over a week to do it."

"Well—you look as if *you'd* been beaten—by a bunch of strong-armed thugs. Why was it so important to beat Charlie?"

"Because he's so darned cocky—that's why. Jerry and Frazier and Donald Manker and some other kids thought it up and planned the whole thing."

"Why didn't Frazier beat him?" Father asked with deliberate denseness. "Frazier's the best player in high school."

"Father!" I groaned. "That wouldn't have meant anything. It had to be me."

"Oh—because you're a girl. I see." Father again used his annoying simple-minded ruse. "Why didn't Helen Fitzgerald take on this Charlie? She's twice the tennis player you are. She could have beaten him without getting apoplexy."

"Oh, for goodness' sake, Father, are you dumb or something? Can't you see how much worse this dope would feel having *me* beat him?"

"I get it." Father sighed deeply. "Well, all I can say is that I'm disappointed in you."

"Disappointed in me! Every single person in this whole town thinks I'm wonderful, that's all!"

"Well, I don't!" Father snapped. "I thought you'd long since decided it wasn't sporting to take advantage of people because of your crutches."

"Father—for heaven's sake, what's the matter with you? I didn't take advantage of him. I beat him fair and square. He played just as hard as he could. The score was twelve-ten—that shows you. The kids called a lot of the shots wrong but I corrected every time in Charlie's favor. And he offered me a fifteen handicap but I threw it right back in his face."

"You certainly salted his wounds, didn't you?"

I stared, incredulous, at Father.

"You know—" Father paused to frown at me. "You present a very complex moral problem and I don't have any good precedents to follow in rearing you properly. But of *this* I am convinced: you took greater advantage of that boy today than if you'd frankly cheated him. You had a physical and personality advantage over him that must have made his defeat insufferable. If he'd beaten you twelve-ten, you'd have walked off the court the victor, just the same."

"That's absolutely silly!" I protested, although this was true and I knew it. We'd counted on just that in our ingenious plot.

"It's complicated, I grant you, but not silly. This isn't complicated, however. I'm glad you can swim and play tennis and ride a horse, but the only reason I'm glad is because these things are fun. That's why you and everyone else is supposed to do them. When you play a game just to demonstrate what hot stuff you are on your crutches, it's time you quit and took up china painting, as your grandmother would have you do. Remember Grandma and your first roller skates? She was afraid you'd join a carnival if you learned to skate. Well—for my money, you were too close to the carnival for comfort today."

"Honestly, Father, you *surprise* me!" I protested even as my mind touched the peculiarly devious truth toward which he was leading me. "I suppose you just never want me to win anything," I continued perversely.

"Of course, I want you to win—but only the game. Now, beat it! Take a bath and go to bed. Get out of my sight. I can't stand you."

I started to cry as I left the room.

"By the way, you must have played inspired tennis today," Father called after me.

"I was hot, all right. I played much better than I am able to play."

"Hum. . . ." Father sighed with what seemed almost wistfulness. "I wouldn't have minded seeing that game."

"You'd have put a stop to it though, I suppose—You and your ideas!"

"That's right," agreed Father, "I would have."

He was furious enough with me to cheerfully shake

out my molars. But at the same time, reluctantly and in spite of himself, he was proud. The ethics of being crippled were, I decided, exceedingly complicated and obscure. But clear enough, nevertheless, that I never bragged to anyone about beating Charlie.

CHAPTER IV

The Leg and I

EVEN before I'd mastered crutches, I was restlessly eager for the day that I'd trot smartly down the street on an artificial leg. Enterprising companies which dealt in mechanical kickers, from Minneapolis to San Francisco, apparently had alert spies in the field, or more probably, they subscribed to clipping bureaus that gave them immediate notice of accidents resulting in amputations. Anyway, before I was well out from under the anesthetic, I was deluged with literature that described some miraculous wares. The family censored my incoming mail to protect me from this advertising matter. However, much of it arrived in plain envelopes and the nurses occasionally slipped up and delivered it to me. Contrary to parental expectation that this material might upset me, it was like most contraband reading and I reveled in it.

I hadn't been home from the hospital very long before slightly limping salesmen began calling on Father. It is customary for artificial limb companies to employ men who can make practical and personal demonstrations.

My parents, like me, had no idea in mind except to get me onto an artificial leg as promptly as possible. It was our complete expectation that I would go through life with two legs—one detachable. Crutches were only a temporary substitute to keep me ambulatory while I waited impatiently for over a year, on the advice of my surgeon, before being fitted.

This delay was undoubtedly unfortunate. It was responsible in great part, I am sure, for the fact that I habitually walk on crutches today. During that year my yellow pine sticks became almost anatomical. For all practical purposes they were as good as grafted under my arms.

However well I walked on crutches, I was still convinced that I would do much better on a leg. I was fretful to get going. Father studied all the brochures carefully, interviewed the salesmen, and solicited impartial advice wherever he could get any. There was only one artificial-leg user in our town, a recently handicapped woman of about fifty-five. Mother and Father called on her but she was not introduced to me because my parents were afraid her ineptitude would discourage me.

I read all the success stories in the advertising pamphlets and gazed with awed admiration on the cuts of legless wonders who endorsed the various appliances. My choice was a concern which claimed as one of their happy customers a cowboy, a one-legger, photographed with two guns attached to his belt. I somehow dreamed up the notion that the guns came, like premiums, with all purchases. It was an appealing misconception and sold me completely on that company.

Father, however, was not as romantically inclined. I grew very impatient with his deliberation. He finally selected an excellent small firm in Oakland, California, to fashion my first prosthesis. They were reliable; their product was sound—even if they couldn't claim any gun-lugging clients. Moreover, Oakland was the most conveniently located city for me to go for fittings. It was only a scant hundred miles away.

A very easy-stepping representative from the company called on us to make preliminary arrangements. He not only was minus a leg—he was minus two. My eyes bulged when he rolled up his trousers and displayed his artificial limbs. No gentleman had ever rolled up his trouser legs in our parlor before. Much more fascinating than his exhibitionism, however, was the fact that he had his socks held up, not with garters, but with thumbtacks. The pleasant picture immediately crossed my mind—me, sitting in the midst of an admiring circle, pounding nails into my leg while my horrified audience waited breathlessly for me to bleed.

The salesman was very much on his timber toes. He was jovial and lively. He even rakishly grabbed my startled sister and waltzed her around the room to some vocal "tum-te-tahs" that were vaguely Strauss-ish.

If this remarkable sprite could cavort so impressively on two artificial legs, what couldn't I do with only one? I visualized myself on a flying trapeze—a member of the Russian Ballet with a fancy professional name like Marca Markavitz—disguised as a brave drummer boy marching off to the wars—a cowgirl with the coveted two guns. . . .

The salesman didn't call my attention to his sites of amputation. He had both his natural knees. Regrettably, the great advantage of a surviving knee is usually skimmed over lightly or ignored when artificial limbs are being advertised or when morale is being lifted by its bootstraps.

A great wave of slick stories has pounded the public recently in which disabled soldiers bounce out of their beds, strap on artificial legs, and promptly dance off with pretty nurses. In one such stirring piece of amazing fiction, I recall a wounded veteran, with some trying complexes and a new wooden leg, who was lured onto the dance floor by a very swish female morale-lifter. She was a magnificent pin-up type, graceful and svelte, and she danced like a veritable Pavlova. She not only affected a miraculous cure of the poor boy's complexes, she practically put blood and bones in his wooden leg. A few days later, the susceptible soldier, cheek to cheek with this Song-of-Bernadette healer, was also tripping the light fantastic like a gilded playboy from a follies extravaganza. Only then did this deceitful slick dish break down shyly, under the influence of moonlight, and confess that she too had an artificial leg. The soldier nearly died of the shock—and even I, who wasn't there and just read the story, threw up!

Lots of people dance on artificial legs and dance well. But the smoothest of these talented unipeds invariably are those who still retain a God-given knee. Whether the authors assigned to whip up these fantasies exaggerate from well-intentioned motive or from ignorance or from both, I don't know. It is much more blasting to morale, however, to discover, only after bitter experience, how superior a real knee is to a mechanical one. In my opinion, it would help rather than hurt morale to point this out.

I reread the story of the one-legged blonde operator—no limper she! I pointed out each word with my index finger and sounded it phonetically—to see if even once the author hinted as to the site of this remarkable girl's amputation. I would have come close to adoring that glamorous heroine—and on feminine principle I'm against glamorous women—if she'd announced with forthright candor, "I've still got my knee, you know, and I'm so astonishingly adept that I don't have so much as a distinguished limp."

Also, I sometimes toss fretfully through the black night speculating about the Yank. He was supposedly terrifically red-blooded American. Didn't he look at her legs? Maybe he had a hollow head, as well as a hollow leg. The author didn't say.

But to return to our parlor demonstrator, he took me out on the lawn and kicked a football way down the street. "That's what you'll be doing one of these days," he assured me. He got much more kick out of his leg, however, than I ever did out of mine.

Inside the house again, he took all my measurements. He traced the shape of my surviving leg as a pattern for my new model. He gave Mother instructions for binding my stump with elasticized bandage—an uncomfortable but apparently necessary procedure for shrinking it to fit the socket of a prosthesis. Father agreed to take me to Oakland for a two-week stay when the appliance neared completion so that the final fitting would be exactly right, and so that I could learn from experts the technique of walking.

Father drove us to Berkeley, where Mother, Bernice, and I were to be the guests of some old friends. Father returned home to keep things going at the office and fill the kitchen sink with dirty dishes.

Every day Mother and I took a trolley ride to the

leg makers in Oakland. It was a fascinating place. Every employee, from the owner down to the lowliest chore boy, wore some sort of a prosthesis. This situation has been common to every orthopedic appliance concern I have visited throughout my lifetime.

When Bernice went with us, she and I played an engrossing game while waiting in the reception room. Whenever anyone—employee or customer—walked through, we tried to beat each other calling the handicaps. "No legs"—"One leg"—"One arm"—we whispered. It was a variation on "Beaver"; twenty points for a legless woman; ten points for a legless man, etc.

My new limb was made of well-seasoned English willow, a material that has apparently proved very successful. Every leg I have ever purchased, from a variety of makers, was contrived of that same wood.

I had presented a right shoe to the manufacturers so that they could build the new foot to size and adjust the ankle mechanism to heel height, but we forgot all about stockings. I habitually wore half socks, and I felt somewhat crestfallen and old-fashioned when Mother dashed out and bought me the long, ribbed white cotton stockings necessary to conceal my new steel joints. My first leg didn't have a hip-control belt. This efficient device was not yet invented and also, I had no consequential hips at the age of ten. I wore a rather complicated over-the-shoulders harness onto which the appliance was fastened by snap hooks.

From the beginning I managed quite well. Every day I paraded up and down a back room at the shop, supporting myself on the hand rods of a walking lane which had a mirror at one end so that I could watch myself. I wasn't particularly impressed. I was surprised that I limped. A very kindly one-legged man who also had a thigh amputation, supervised me. I tended to throw my leg stiffly offside, avoiding the complication of the knee. Patiently, he taught me to maintain proper posture and how to swing the leg to facilitate the knee motion.

I was finally permitted to wear the leg back to Berkeley, although I used my crutches as safety props on the trip, and we went by taxi rather than trolley. Although everyone was delighted with my aptitude and progress, we were advised to remain in Berkeley a few more days to be certain that no hip or groin pain developed to indicate an improper fit.

For practice, every morning I walked round and round the dining-room table, an excellent training place since the table edge served as an emergency support. Every afternoon Bernice and I went out for a little walk. If I grew tired, she put an arm around me as an auxiliary aid on the way home. It became easier every day, and our expeditions were daily farther afield. I figured with unwarranted optimism that it was only a matter of time before the leg would begin running with me.

One afternoon we were on our usual stroll through the university campus when an "unusual" California rain began to fall. We were in danger of being drenched, and since my leg hadn't yet started to run, our progress was slow and laborious. In hurrying, I slipped precariously on the pavement. The new knee was cutting perverse capers.

My sister had on a new and very becoming pink challis dress. Bernice was fifteen and very pretty and consequently thought constantly about her appearance. "My dress will be ruined!" she yowled.

"I'll tell you what!" I was inspired. "I'll take off the leg and hop home." I was an old hand—or rather, an old foot—at hopping.

Providentially, the streets were pretty well deserted, since sensible pedestrians had all sought shelter. Against her better judgment, Bernice, who was a strict conformist, agreed. I hid behind some bushes, lifted up my dress, and unhooked my hindrance. Shades of a good sadistic ax murder—Bernice then slung the very realistic stockinged and shoed leg over her shoulder! She glanced furtively in all directions, and we started home as briskly as the somewhat unusual circumstances permitted.

We must have presented a startling picture. Certainly the staring astonished policeman at our first street crossing looked as if he'd just had a run-in with a ghost.

Not by design, I am sure, but by sheer confusion, he chose his perfect lines. "What's coming off around here?" he demanded gruffly.

Bernice, in her acute embarrassment, promptly dropped her encumbrance. It was her first guilty encounter with The Law.

The policeman leaned down and warily touched the leg before picking it up. "Thank the Holy Mother —it's wood!" he said. His breath smelled somewhat peculiar, which may have had some bearing on his next and, to us, incomprehensible speech. "Cold day, you know. Been trying to keep warm—but no matter. This break off or something?"

Bernice explained fully and apologetically while her pink dress wilted in the rain.

The policeman propped my leg against a wall and put us under a store awning. He then talked into one of those fascinating boxed phones attached to a light post. In a few minutes a Black Maria pulled up at the curb. Bernice and I were chauffeured home at the city's expense.

Not being a shy little mite, even caught out with my leg off, I suggested to the driver that it would be nice if he blew his siren and also made a little better time.

"O.K., kid," he agreed cheerfully. "This don't happen

every day on my beat. I expect you could call it an emergency."

With satisfactory fanfare, we sped through the quiet Berkeley streets.

"Isn't it lucky I took off my leg?" I whispered to Bernice. "I always wanted to ride in a police car. Let's try it in Oakland tomorrow, shall we?"

"Oh, *Louise!*" my sister gasped. "I'm going to tell Mama on you. You are a very wicked little girl."

For this, I suppose, there was no really sound argument. Since that day, I've never ridden behind a siren. Nevertheless, there's my formula for turning the trick. And like any ethical scientist, I hereby present it to the world.

CHAPTER V

Off with Her Leg

HOME again, I called in all the neighborhood gang to see the new leg and listen to me brag about our Berkeley adventures. However, the new kicker was only a one-day wonder, since it wasn't something that could be passed around for everyone to ride on.

I limped off to school on the following Monday, without so much as a cane. I was an exceptionally good walker, but walking was the only thing of consequence I ever accomplished on the leg. I no longer went places in a dashing hurry, and either I or the leg stayed home when long hikes, or fishing in the creek, were the attractions of the day.

Although Grandma sighed her pleasure and said, "She looks like a little lady now. We may even be able to marry her off when she grows up," to me, the only tangible advantage of the leg was that I had my arms free. When I swatted a baseball, I was able to put much more umph into it than I had on the more restraining crutches. However, I now suffered the indignity of having someone run bases for me. The attachment was superbly adapted to volley ball which requires little active leg work but lots of aerial defense.

Whenever a new child showed up at grammar school I startled him goggle-eyed by pushing thumbtacks into my leg. (Mother refused to let me use nails and a hammer. After all, the leg represented a substantial investment of about one hundred and twenty-five dollars.) I could also slip my stump out of the leg's socket and twine the leg around my neck. This was good box office, and I often did a routine of grotesque contortions that passed in my social circle for very accomplished eccentric dancing.

For a while the new leg accentuated to the point of real discomfort my "phantom limb." This is a curious sensation that most amputees experience in various degrees. The stimulation of the sensory nerves in the stump results in the sensation that the amputated member is still there.

I was in the hospital when I first felt the phantom limb. It didn't, however, astonish me in the least. I had just recently made a prayerful suggestion to Jesus, whom I knew by reputation to be very good at miracles and tremendously compassionate of even a poor small sparrow's suffering. I thought He might oblige by doing a small job for me along the line of spontaneous regeneration. When I felt my toes under the sheets—

somewhat numb and prickly as if they'd been sat on too long but nevertheless there—I rang for the nurse. I asked her to pull back the blankets for me to see.

"My leg just grew back," I announced without taxing my faith a whit. After all, this wasn't anywhere near as big a job as bringing back Lazarus.

"Poor, poor little dear—no," she said.

"Oh, yes," I assured her. "Jesus did it."

That was when I learned about the phantom limb and revised my expectations for divine intervention.

Off and on, I felt it in varying degrees. It usually accompanied fatigue, and I could also feel it merely by thinking about my missing extremity. The sensation was almost constant, however, during the first few weeks I wore the new leg. It was so realistic that, without thinking, I frequently leaned down and scratched my prickly pseudo-toes.

In a very short time this uncomfortable phase passed, and the new limb gave me neither psychological nor physical distress of any kind. I can still summon my specter, but it rarely comes uncalled.

In other ways the leg was well behaved. Nothing mechanical went wrong that a screw driver or an oil can couldn't promptly remedy.

Then, after only three months, my mother noticed that my right shoulder was sagging. It wasn't the leg's fault. I was growing—and like a weed apparently. Off we went to Oakland, where I was once more measured carefully. We left the leg to be lengthened. Even for adult users, it is a great advantage to live in a city large enough to support an artificial leg shop where quick and efficient service is always available for repairs and adjustments.

The leg was in Oakland three weeks, during which interim I went back to the more lively crutches. This was the first step in my reversion. When the leg returned by express I gave it a rather frosty welcome, but I donned it again.

The lengthening had been done in the shank only, and a solid rather than a hollow piece had been inserted. The result was a much heavier load than I was accustomed to. Also, as a consequence of extending only the lower leg, the over-all device wasn't quite properly proportioned aesthetically to my natural leg. I wasn't satisfied, but I wore it.

In a few months, my posture was once more beginning to show mild distortion. The local shoemaker helped me temporarily by putting a slight raise on the right shoe sole. But Nature being as one-tracked as she is, I kept right on growing.

When another alteration was again inevitable, Father decided after consultation with factory experts that I'd better have a completely new leg. The family budget had to be revised to accommodate itself to two legs a year instead of one. Father was an ill-paid social worker. I know that both he and Mother went without new winter coats to compensate for this added expense, but they never admitted it nor begrudged it. They would have mortgaged our house gladly, I am sure, so that I could luxuriate in new legs.

Two weeks in Oakland appealed to me much more than the prospect of sporting the new model. The handwriting was already on the wall but we were all too stubbornly attached to our preconceived notions to read it.

For another year the warfare waged between my physical growth and my leg's inelasticity—with my active athletic ambitions throwing their weight in with my physical growth. With each lapse in use, during the leg's necessary absences in Oakland for repairs or lengthening, I grew more attached to my crutches. Finally, I pleaded with my parents to let me abandon the appliance completely. They agreed, and we hung it on a nail in the garage, not knowing the proper disposal of a defunct leg. There it stayed for years—coming into prominence only on very rare occasions when we children used it as a prop in some macabre bits of imaginative play.

It was indispensable in a "mystifying" magic performance in which I was a full financial partner with a little tow-headed boy, Chadwick Augustus Barnes, named for an admirable relative on his mother's side who happened to own a bank. Chadwick's friends called him Gus and his enemies called him Fish Face.

He looked like the banker. Gus was the brains of our corporation. He wore a big black mustache and did card tricks inherited from his father, a famous parlor bore. He also turned water into unpalatable wine, with the help of a Junior Chemical Set, presented to him one Christmas by his aunt who lived in Detroit, well removed from the foul smells her generosity stirred up in California. It was during the high point of Gus's Houdini buffoonery that I figured and earned my half of the pins and pennies. This was a modest variation of the sawing of the beautiful damsel in twain. Gus sawed off my leg—or at any rate he made sawing motions, accompanied by an effective buzzing noise which, in his cleverness, he could accomplish without moving his mouth. He then effected the severance. Of course, this never fooled our audience any more than the card tricks fooled them, but they always savored the savage artistry of Gus's technique and my own dramatic contribution which consisted of anguished groans and wails.

My mother didn't exactly condone this hanky-panky but she tolerated it in the name of harmless childish fun. However, she drew a firm line and withdrew the leg from its promising theatrical career following another little drama in which it was featured.

There was a bad three-car smashup on the highway south of town one afternoon. Although I was perishing to run down there and get a glimpse of the gore, I was not permitted to. Mother had the strange aberration that such things weren't proper sights for a nice little girl. The aberration, of course, was that I was a nice little girl.

"You just never let me have *any* fun, Mama," I complained.

"You have plenty of fun," Mother said.

Goodness! I did too. By the end of the day I had had so much fun, I took my spanking stoically and still figured I'd had the best of the bargain.

Several of the brighter boys on our block outwitted their parents and did get a look at the demolished cars. Regrettably, the bodies, both live and dead, had been removed. These delightful little lads came back from the wreck with their imaginative scheme. It was beautiful and appealed thoroughly to my fine, sensitive nature.

We worked in Father's respectable garage performing our grim task. We dressed my leg in an old white stocking and shoe. We borrowed a bottle of catsup from Mother, without a by-her-leave, and splattered it liberally over the stocking. Then we stowed this charming "souvenir of the accident" into a carton and lugged it around the neighborhood, displaying it as something we just happened to see lying by the roadside at the scene of the crash.

Of course, my leg was fairly prominent locally, but even so, on this occasion it invariably brought forth a feminine scream and a double-take before it was recognized. Several slightly neurotic ladies were somewhat upset over the proceedings and made their disquietude known to my mother.

The only irony in this story is that I was the only participant who was spanked. No matter what trouble that leg ever got itself into, I had to take the rap.

Had I been adult when my accident occurred—or even sixteen—I probably would have walked gracefully and happily through life with the constant help and the aesthetic advantage of an artificial leg. Certainly I approve of them, and I really wish this had been the case. As it was, the best prosthesis in the world simply wasn't able to keep up with me. It is regretful that those youthful years on crutches set this situation into a permanent pattern. I have worn legs since then. According to the manufacturers, I walked exceptionally well. I have even been called upon to demonstrate on a few occasions for discouraged users. I make this boast not out of vanity but merely to point out that it isn't any sane reason that keeps me off an artificial leg. On a leg I feel conspicuous and crippled. On crutches I don't. I ought to have my head examined.

CHAPTER VI

The Road to Buenos Aires

EARLY in my teens our family migrated from the San Joaquin Valley to Los Angeles where Father was offered a much better job. None of us wanted to go. Father could orate stirringly, at the drop of any expensive suggestion, on the subject, "Money Isn't Important." My sister and I habitually took him to task for this flimsy whimsy. But when *we* brought up his old saw about money being just negligible green stuff, as a supporting argument against moving, Father got very tight-lipped. In rebuttal, he offered another of his quaint lectures—"The Educational Opportunities for My Daughters." Frankly, I suspect Father changed positions for no reason more complicated than the more comfortable weight of his new pay envelope. Since he was in the service of humanity, however, such heresy was never hinted.

Whatever the reason, Los Angeles became our new home. It was for me, anyway, a very difficult adjustment. I was no longer a novelty in our small town. Everyone was accustomed to me and my crutches and knew my complete history right back to Mother's first labor pain. But here was a huge city of strangers, all staring at me, or so I surmised. My surmise was not too exaggerated either, for the more curious often stopped me on the street and made blatant inquiry. "My poor girl, whatever happened to you?"

Strange men offered me rides. I am sorry to admit that probably not one of these misunderstood gentlemen had so much as a mild flutter of bad intention toward me. In my middy blouse marching myself to high school on my crutches, I am pretty sure I didn't set the baser instincts spinning. Having been warned, however, that a city man behind the wheel of an automobile was definitely not the same cozy dish of tea that my father was, I always went into a panic when a car pulled to the curb and some harmless man stuck a head out and yelled, "Little girl, can't I drive you to school?" I refused always, just as promptly as my chattering jaws would allow, and at the same time I backed off down the street as fast as I could navigate in reverse.

I was so accustomed to treatment exactly like that accorded all the other boys and girls in our town that it didn't occur to me that I was singled out for gratuitous transportation because I was crippled. This was surely the evil city I'd been warned against.

With some reticence I finally broached the delicate problem to my sister, who was by this time a very worldly freshman at U.S.C. I dared not mention it to Mother who supposedly had known the facts of life for some time but was still acutely embarrassed over them.

"Are the white slavers after you, too?" I began timidly.

"*Louise!*" My sister grabbed my shoulder and shook me in her horrified astonishment. "What are you saying? Of course they aren't after me! What do you mean?" She paused in her tirade long enough to reassure herself by looking me up and down. "They *could*n't be after *you!*"

Bernice didn't often give me her unwavering attention, but I had it now. "Yes, they are *so* after me," I insisted with just a touch of pride. "And you'd better believe it, so there!" I proceeded to tell her how almost every day some sinister fiend, disguised in respectable pin-stripe or navy serge, pulled up and offered me a ride.

Bernice released her breath with a long, relieved sigh.

"Do women ever offer you rides?" she demanded, completely calm again.

"Oh, yes—sometimes women offer me rides, too. I get in with *them.* They drive me to school."

"Did it ever occur to you that maybe the men want to drive you to school too, you little goose?"

"Oh, they say they do—but I wasn't born yesterday."

I squinted my eyes to give the impression of vast sophistication.

Bernice proceeded thoroughly to blast my ego. "It's because of your crutches, silly. They're just being nice to you."

"Oh, my goodness!" I gasped, remembering with embarrassment the awful imprecations I had heaped on several innocent heads. It suddenly seemed so simple. "I might as well ride then, I suppose."

"Oh, no!" Bernice said firmly. "Better not ride. Heaven knows, I think you're quite safe." It didn't sound flattering the way she put it. "Still there are some queer characters in the world. Just say, 'No, thank you,' but for goodness' sake, be polite about it!"

The very next day a man offered me a ride, and in consequence of his kindly insight, made a great contribution to both my transportation problem and my popularity. He pulled up, tendered his invitation, and was refused—this time with elaborate courtesy.

"Your mother doesn't let you ride with strangers, does she?" he asked. "I don't blame her either, but I go directly by your school and I'd very much like to give you a lift. See those boys coming down the street there? Do you know them?"

I was too new to *know* anybody. "No," I admitted, "but that middle one's the captain of the football team at high school."

"If I offer them a ride too and they get in, will you?

I'm a frail fellow and those three lads can finish me off thoroughly, if I get fresh." He laughed.

This was the first of my would-be abductors that I'd ever paused to study. He didn't look the least bit like a disguised procurer. As a matter of fact, he looked very nice although not as exciting as his predecessors who I had imagined were tapping me for the life of shame.

"Hey, fellows!" he yelled. "How's about a ride to school?"

They came running and leaped in. I got in, too, still a bit wary. The trip wasn't the Road to Buenos Aires, however. We were deposited without mortal struggle at the high school.

From then on the captain of the football team said "Hi" whenever we met. It helped my social standing, as a newcomer, no end.

When I told Father about this, without elaborating on my former experiences with the white slavers, he gave me permission to ride with strangers who would pick up a whole carload.

From then on, whenever a driver stopped and offered me a ride, I suggested that he also take whatever boys and girls were near by on the sidewalk. He was always amenable. Before very long no one was more popular as a walking companion than I. It was actually the way I first got acquainted in high school.

The years from fourteen to eighteen are probably the darkest ones that a handicapped person must struggle through. Adolescence is not only a period of mercurial moods, it is also a period of great conformity. Any deviation from the norm is felt most acutely at this time in life. A batch of schoolgirls are likely to be almost monotonous in their similarity. If an oversize man's shirt with the tails flapping in the breeze is the chic rage of the hour, all the girls promptly rig themselves out in such monstrosities. If "wizard" is the momentarily approved adjective and anything exciting is supposed to "send you," all adolescent girls recite by rote, "It's wizard"—"It sends me." They only feel secure in complete conformity. It is much later that the equally strong urge for individuality develops. So—during my adolescence I suffered inwardly because crutches weren't sufficiently fashionable to start a wave of amputations.

The weight of my crutch-born individuality was heavy upon me. However, if I had only recognized the fact, it served me well. I was easy to identify. I could never have been a Pinkerton operator, but no one who met me once, forgot me—not because of my memorable personality and my ravishing beauty, but because of my crutches. In one semester in that large metropolitan high school of some four thousand students, I became almost as well known as the best quarter-back. I was also friendly by nature and became a sure thing on a political ticket.

I began to be nominated and elected to all kinds of school and club offices. Practically everyone knew my name and was on speaking terms with me. Also, I had the solid political support of all the smooth girls in school. They were willing to vote for me because they liked me, of course, but also heavily weighted in my favor was the fact that I was no Menace. They figured I'd never beat their time with any of the boys who rated sufficiently to serve with me on the Student Council. I am not obtuse enough to insist that my crutches alone made me "The People's Choice" but I do know they had a great deal to do with it.

This tendency for success in student politics carried right through college. I got quite a reputation for being executive. Actually, I was about as executive as a spring fryer trying to outwit the man with the ax. I didn't actually yank myself out of this compensatory political bingeing until I was mature enough to see the horrible humor in Helen Hokinson's cartoons. I decided I'd better pull myself together or I'd turn out to be a "club dowager" or worse yet, a Congresswoman—and then, God save America! Now, even under the unscrupulous spell of a hypnotist, I don't believe my well-behaved tongue would say "Yes," if someone asked me to serve temporarily as sixteenth alternate on an unimportant subcommittee.

But in high school, dashing about managing things helped me a great deal psychologically. I was president of one thing or another twelve times before I graduated. But the sad truth was—I would much rather have been "right" than president. I was all wrong.

Adolescent boys are precisely the conformists that adolescent girls are. My male classmates all picked carbon copies for girl friends. At the age when the height of achievement is leading a prom grand march with a gangly pimpled youth, I was a great gal with the gavel. It wasn't adequate compensation. I was pretty enough, all Grandmother's direst prophecies to the contrary. My wardrobe was tasteful and adequate and magnificently reinforced by illegal pirating of my sister's closet. So far as I know, I had none of the awful afflictions that advertisers lead one to believe make wallflowers out of glamour girls. However, I led the sort of life that prompted Mother to say, "Isn't it wonderful that Louise isn't boy crazy? Remember Bernice at that age? My goodness, we couldn't sweep the place clean of boys. Louise is so sensible."

Dear Mama! I was about as sensible as a Mongolian idiot. I was just as boy crazy as Bernice, but I was infinitely more frustrated since I didn't have Bernice's reassuring following.

Oh, I got my hand squeezed a few times. Boys took me to the movies occasionally and played tennis with me, and I regularly helped several classy dunderheads with their homework. A couple of boys even kissed me when I was sixteen, but one of these was a Lothario who made a bet that he would kiss every girl in the senior class who didn't have eczema or buck teeth. And with the other, I suspect, kissing was a reflex action that came automatically with the words "good night." I was just a "dandy pal"—a nauseating phrase—to the boys. I even maneuvered dates for them with the ladies of their choice. But I wasn't the least bit pleased with my "wholesome relationships." For all the good it did me, moonlight might have been an impractical invention of the Mazda Lamp Company. I certainly would have had one hell of a time becoming a juvenile delinquent.

"Make her practice her music lessons," Grandma used to say. "Or teach her stenography. She'll never get a man." I took my second husband out to Grandmother's grave a couple of years ago, just to show her! I heard Grandma rotating like a whirling dervish.

However, in my teens I shared Grandma's grimmest expectations. I decided to be an intellectual—the toast of Bohemian salons! I even took to writing poetry—a charitable way of putting it. My effusions were of the "Oh, Love, let us flee—our souls are stifling" school. I read books—uninteresting, uplifting, deep ones, with now and then a detective story tossed in, just to keep me in tune with the world. I would much rather have misspent my youth in riotous living.

But, like a lot of bad-tasting medicine, all this dosage resulted in eventual good. The reading made a permanent impression on me. More important at the time—or so it seemed to me—I got a masculine following! The long hairs, who likewise had stifled souls, began taking an interest in me. They were mostly pasty-faced lads who just *despised* football. They got straight *A* averages in school but ran to drooping shoulders from carrying heavy books, and thick glasses from eye strain. I'd have traded them, three to one, for a really dangerous muscle-bound deadhead. However, at sixteen, a girl on crutches counts her blessings by quantity not quality.

"I wonder where those boy friends of yours go at night?" my sister once asked. "Into dank holes? I bet they weren't born either—I bet they were spawned."

"You're just jealous!" I raged. "Just because nobody ever admired *your* mind. They are brilliant, misunderstood boys. They are stifled—" I ran down suddenly and faced reality. "Oh, Bernice—do you think, with only one leg, I'll ever get a really wonderful man without brains?"

CHAPTER VII

Some Horses and a Husband

IN DUE time I had a high school diploma proudly clutched in my hot little hand. As questionable reward for an honorable scholastic record, I was permitted to stand up on the stage on graduation day and deliver myself of my uplifting opinions. The general gist of the soul-stirring oration was, "Face life squarely." Recited in the safe security of the family circle, my collection of clichés clocked off three minutes to the second, the precise time allotted to present my philosophy to the public. However, on commencement day, I distinguished myself by winning some kind of a record and poured out my memorized sentiments in jive time—finishing in one minute flat. I suspect that my listeners went forth inspired to face life on the bias.

To make the adjustment to higher learning as easy as possible for me, my parents packed me off to Pomona, a good, small, coeducational college in a country town. Father, with his usual studied approach to a problem, digested the brochures of countless colleges and universities and carefully selected one with high academic standing, high moral tone, and no sororities. He was afraid I might not be bid to a sorority and would consequently have my life warped.

By the time I was seventeen, however, it would have been hard to warp my life. I had tossed off most of my adolescent complexes and so, apparently, had my contemporaries. In college—such is my trusting opinion, anyway—I stood pretty solidly on my own personality, without either excess support or excess unbalance from my crutches.

I was no raring, tearing charmer, but I don't mind saying I even began appealing to brainless men. In fact, Father says that for a year or so there, he doesn't think I had a nibble from anyone with an I.Q. over seventy—judging by their conversations.

But, being completely perverse, I promptly started admiring mentality, a tendency that got completely out of hand, in fact. During my junior year at the age of nineteen, I fell flat on my face, with frightful coronary symptoms, for a professor. He never had a peaceful moment, poor man, until I had him at the altar three years later. From then on—he never had a peaceful moment until he escaped via the divorce court.

He was such a nice man, quite undeserving of his fate. A British colonial, born in Burma, he looked, to my misty eyes anyway, exactly like Clive of India (à la Ronald Colman). He made some lasting contributions to me for which he got little substantial return. His mother gave me her magnificent recipe for Indian curry, and he, being not only proper British but also a professor of English, reformed my manners and my grammar considerably. He also taught me a couple of colorful bad words in Burmese and Hindustani.

From my encounter with him, I also learned the comforting fact that no one dies of a broken heart. Put together and given a reasonable rest cure, an old ticker will get you into almost as much fascinating trouble as a brand-new one.

I must have left some sort of an impression on him, too. I know I improved his taste in neckties, and apparently I didn't embitter him permanently against amputees. After our divorce, anyway, he started beauing a one-armed woman.

Grandma couldn't get over my snagging a man, and she thought I ought to be committed to an institution when I let him off the hook. "What are you thinking of!" she gasped. "What did they teach you in college? You ought to know that lightning never strikes twice in the same place. Besides," she added as a pious but unconvincing afterthought, "divorces are wicked. Still—he isn't a citizen. That would have parted you eventually. Kings and such like—always having to call on God to save them."

Exactly what Grandma meant I am not sure. She was an isolationist. It was her studied opinion that only sixth-generation Americans were admitted to Heaven, and even then, it helped outwit the red tape at the Gate if they happened to be her blood kin.

On registration day at college, the head of the women's physical education department made me a tempting offer. "Would you like to sign up for an hour of rest every day, in place of required physical education courses? We'll allocate full credit."

Today if such a pleasant proposition were put to me, I would not only say "yes" without hesitation, I'd bring my own pillow and offer to major in the subject. But since I was still a little huffy about myself, I assured her that with some leeway in selection I could undoubtedly fulfill my physical education requirements, if not to the letter, at least to the spirit of the law. Skipping formal gymnastics and team sports—which all my friends regarded as rank privilege—I concentrated on swimming, riflery, archery, tennis, and riding. With the exception of tennis, the limitations of which I have explained, all these sports were very well adapted to my abilities. I captained my class swimming team and earned part of my more frivolous expenses at college, life-guarding the girls' swimming pool during open hours. I was also on the archery team.

In riflery I was mediocre and did fairly well only in the prone position. If I were ever threatened by a fiend and had a rifle handy, I'd have to ask him politely to wait to be shot until I flung myself flat on my stomach.

I never approximated the career of National Velvet, but horseback riding became my favorite recreational activity. Prior to college, I was on cozy terms with one burro and two kindly but senile retired horses owned by a rancher friend of ours. Freshman year, however, I signed up for riding classes. Miss Margaret Pooley, the instructress, had never confronted a problem like me, but she was imaginative and took a very kindly interest in working out a technique that made allowances for my physical limitations. Under her guidance, I developed an equestrian skill that gave the impression of good form while breaking most of the time-honored rules of horsemanship.

Also during that first year, thanks to my friendship with Marion Cox, an Arizona girl, who I suspect could talk to horses in their own language, I fell into the Horsy Set. This bunch of boys and girls, many of them from Western ranches, and some of them just crazy on purpose, practically slept with their boots on. They took me in hand.

I think we'd gladly have occupied box stalls and munched a straight diet of oats. We arose at odd and inhuman hours and rode before breakfast, and blissfully we cantered around in the moonlight. We wore our riding clothes right into the sacred halls of learning. I suspect we smelled habitually like an essence that Saks Fifth would probably call "Fatal Stable" or "L'Amour Equin." Saturdays we made worshipful pilgrimages to various near-by horsey meccas—Carnation Farm Stables, Kellogg's Arabian Horse Farm, Diamond Bar Ranch, etc. We weren't even on nodding terms with any of the owners of California's flashy horseflesh, but we were chummy with all the grooms. We were privileged to pat some very aristocratic flanks. When a horse show was scheduled anywhere in Southern California, our little crew, without owning so much as a Shetland pony between us, usually had exhibitors' badges and occupied complimentary boxes. These were presented to us by some softhearted hostler who figured I'd never be able to climb up on the grandstand. None of us discouraged such gentle instincts. In fact, I could go becomingly fragile whenever the situation seemed to demand it—sighing and lifting my crutches wearily, as if they weighed two tons apiece. Father would have slain me.

Riding is an excellent sport for an amputee although it does necessitate special techniques. To start with, there's the elementary problem of getting on the horse. I usually mount by having some friendly weight-lifter give me a leg up. Frequently I use an orthodox box; or with one supporting crutch, I can step my foot into the stirrup and swing up. The flashiest way for a uniped to mount is with a flying leap—in the manner of a cowboy in a *B* Western. I never was able to do this impressive little stunt on anything higher than a pony.

One-legged and crutchless, once in the saddle, I stay there (Heaven helping) until my ride is over, unless accompanied by a stalwart companion, ready to assist on the remount. It is impractical to carry along a crutch.

I have no knee grip. Posting a trot, therefore, is not a sound practice. I learned to approximate the rhythm and made a poor pretense at posting by lifting my weight from my one stirrup. Probably the most sensible management of the trot is to abandon the flat saddle and ride a Stock or a McClellan and sit the gait, cowboy style.

Even better is to ride any saddle—English, Army, or Western—but put it on a five-gaited horse and then rack or canter, avoiding the trot altogether. Now and again a so-called "slow-gaited" horse, a natural single-footer, turns up. That is a splendid mount for a one-legged rider, especially for a beginner who can't cope with the stylish intelligence about signals that usually characterizes a five-gaited horse.

So, pick a single-footer or a five-gaiter, but always make careful preliminary survey of his withers and spine. A one-legger requires a horse with a good sturdy ridge for a backbone. If not, the saddle tends to slip when all the body weight is supported in one stirrup instead of divided between two. Every stable boy who confronts a Single-boot for the first time will argue this point, as he leads out his most dejected nag. An obviously handicapped person always has to fight for a decent mount. I have ridden some bizarre plugs, jovially called "horses" by their custodians. The uninitiated groom will invariably insist, "The way I cinch a saddle, it *can't* slip." Hah—many a saddle cinched so it *can't* slip has gone perverse all of a sudden and slid off, taking me right along with it!

However, a nice sedate easy-gaited horse with a backbone that will hold a saddle reliably can give an amputee a good safe ride. The extra stirrup should be removed, for when it bounces against the horse's flanks it is likely to make him nervous. Also it is just as well to avoid double reins. Both a curb and a snaffle require two hands. It is better practice to use just a curb, and handle the reins in one hand, leaving the other free for that most ignominious breach-of-riding etiquette—pulling leather. Making quick turns at a canter is likely to upset balance. It is far less degrading to push on the saddle with a free hand to maintain equilibrium than it is to fly off into space. Space is notoriously solid at the bottom, as I know from coming down hard on it many times.

An amputee who is bright in the head leaves all

fancy work on horseback to bipeds. It is half-witted for even a normal person to show off on a horse, and it is stark madness for a one-legger. I know—I'm a reformed maniac myself.

In returning to the campus stables from the bridle paths in the foothills, we went directly by the college inn and the dormitories. Since these two blocks were paved, we weren't, of course, permitted to flash by at a canter. Sensibly enough, we were required to walk our horses in this rather populated and busy area. This being a pretty poky regulation, allowing no opportunity to startle bystanders, some of us had a rather wicked little trick for enlivening things. We made clicking noises deep in our throats and at the same time kept the horses' heads reined high. This precarious practice excited our mounts into lifting their hooves prettily, prancing and dancing sideways. We thereby gave the impression to the awed pedestrians on the safe sidewalks, of magnificent management of a herd of wild stallions recently roped on the open range.

One day I rode through this parading ground alone and, as usual, I did my quiet bit of ventriloquism. My horse, normally gentle and long suffering, decided apparently that the time had come, not only to tell me off but to throw me off. He opened his mouth, showed his dentures, and whinnied a noisy impertinent remark that even I who can't speak "horse" understood perfectly. "O.K., smarty-pants, you asked for it!"

He lifted up his rear end three times, and I described a parabola in the air and landed on my fanny, in the middle of an intersection. Man's best friend then turned his head and with a brief horselaugh, hot-hoofed it for the stables. Wise guy—he knew that even if I could catch him, I couldn't remount. If only I had been blessed with a nice little concussion at that point and had collapsed into a comfortable coma, everything would have been dandy. But not me! Except for a certain indelicate numbness that implied I might have a lost weak end, I wasn't wounded a whit.

Anyone else could have arisen and fled the scene of such ignominy—but although I arose, there I stood on one foot. To hop away, flapping my wings like an embittered bird, would only have heaped hot clinkers on my already flaming embarrassment.

People screamed. Old ladies and gents leaped out of their rocking chairs on the porch of the inn, and students raced across the campus. I didn't even have the virtue of being funny. Nobody laughed except one dear, *dear* friend who went into a rollicking display of disgusting good cheer. I felt like Old Hogan's Goat tied to the railroad track, seeing all those chugging rescuers closing in on me.

Not one of them shouted with outrage, "That dangerous wild bronco threw her!"—which, God forgive, he did technically. It was like a horrible ghostly visitation of my old roller-skating days. All the good people lamented in chorus, "That poor, poor girl fell off!"

Just in the nick of time I was spirited away. A car came toward me, and with all the *savoir-faire* of a confirmed hobo, I flung out my thumb. The car braked to a stop and I hopped in.

"Hiyah, Babe," the stranger said, and leered at me. He wasn't local talent. He looked like a graduate of Alcatraz, now that I ponder on his charms, but at that moment he was Galahad on a white charger. When I got to the stables, the horse was quietly munching hay. When he saw me, however, he paused long enough to laugh his fool head off.

"That'll learn her!" he remarked ungrammatically to a mare in the next stall. He was right, too—it learned me good—but he got his come-uppance. He didn't get to finish his vitamins. The stable boy, to discipline both me and the horse, promptly hoisted me up on him again, and I walked sedately back by the inn. I didn't hand him my usual line of deep-throated chatter this time, however. In fact, my conversational wit with horses from that day hence has been limited to "Nice horsy! Nice horsy!"

When I wasn't out courting the horses or compromising the faculty, I did the usual things that lead to an A.B. degree. My major academic interests were in sociology and in English. I figured I'd do the world good with one and do myself good with the other. I didn't distinguish myself scholastically. When the faculty members sit around on a cold winter's night nostalgically reminiscing about students who have made their years of teaching richly worth while, my name is not mentioned. I am more generous with them. When I sit around on cold winter nights reminiscing about the teachers who have influenced my life, there are several, that I didn't even marry, who always come in for praise. In spite of the recorder's office's convincing evidence to the contrary, I got quite a bit out of college.

During those four years I learned a good many odds and ends that were not in the curriculum but which helped me to get ahead in the world. For one thing, it was in college that I quit buying stockings.

My roommate, Lucile Hutton, pointed out that she regarded me as something of a simple sucker for investing in hosiery when I could just as well beg castoffs from my friends. Whenever she got a run in one of a good pair, she presented me with the odd stocking. She very kindly spread the word around the dormitory and before long there were so many contributions, I never purchased any stockings myself. I doubt if I have bought more than half a dozen pairs of hose since. I am quite definitely spoiled. When emergencies have forced me to support my leg in the manner to which it has become accustomed, I have greatly resented the expenditure. During the war when even rayons were hoarded like jewels, I resembled a Black Marketeer. From Pearl Harbor to V-J Day, my leg remained a prewar aristocrat. I wore nylons. Suddenly stocking-conscious, my friends from all over the country sent me their last odd, surviving sheer.

During college I also learned that it was sharp to send my boy friends off to the dances with other women—even when they perjured themselves by swearing their eternal faithfulness to me. Prom night in a girls' dormitory can be a bit grim for a handicapped person. I used to flutter about hooking slinky dresses, powdering bare backs, and pinning on corsages and acting just horribly ecstatic about everyone dashing off without me, for a large evening. Along with a smattering of unlovelies, I was dependably free on the evenings of dances and so I usually operated the dormitory switchboard and let all the late home-comers in the front door. This was a neat device for checking up on what hour my own beau deposited his partner.

My insistence that my current follower date someone else on these evenings did not surge from a noble nature. I didn't subscribe to the theory that virtue is its own reward and that I could have myself a high old time making others happy. It was sound technique. I could dance a little on one crutch, but only a partner who had practiced with me in private could make any real showing in public. At a dance I was a misfit and I knew it, but I never allowed anyone to get the idea that he was saddled with a burden who limited his pleasures. Often overly zealous devotion prompted some unsuspecting young man to make the supreme gesture. When my insistence finally convinced him he should go with someone else, he would ask me for a suggestion as to whom he should date.

Then I exercised my greatest generosity. I always carefully selected someone who might possibly have been a pretty baby, who was known to be good to her mother, and who would make someone, who had sense enough to recognize sterling virtues, a splendid little helpmate. Who could complain about that? There is often more to an ugly mug than meets the eye, I always say, and what's a lumpy figure anyway if it harbors a heart of gold?

I went to college during that dangerous period in the late twenties when easy money, Prohibition, and a hideous collegiate philosophy were madly dancing around, hand in hand. "It's not the grades you make but the college life and the contacts that are important." That little ditty, I am sure, made many a natural *A* student shift into *C* out of sheer apology, and it abetted me in my already deplorable habit of running for office.

Our college town was fresh out of fleshpots, however. It reeked of wholesomeness. Besides, I didn't have enough money to be artistically madcap. My family has always cleverly managed to be respectably poor, even in times of great national prosperity. The only relative we ever had who accumulated an impressive pile of cash was an industrious great-uncle. He was lavishly rewarded with riches for being a vestryman on Sundays, and weekdays paying starvation wages to his employees and working them ten hours, in a cozy place said to resemble the Black Hole of Calcutta. He became something of a baron.

However, he got nervous about his hope for Heaven or else so annoyed with his kin, who looked lustfully eager every time he sneezed, that when finally he died, at the tantalizing age of ninety-two, he left his ill-gotten gains to the church. With proper sentiment, he did preserve for his posterity the family Bible, some bad paintings of grim ancestors, and a silver tea service. I got the tea service, which I must admit was preferable to the ancestors, but even it turned out to be quadruple plate, not sterling. So—I was pretty well imbued with the knowledge that life was real, life was earnest and knew that the minute I graduated from college, I'd have to stand on my own two crutches and dig into my own pocket for small change.

Although I was occasionally lured onto some rather distracting bypaths during my college years, I was fairly well oriented to the straight road to occupational preparation. I am grateful that no one with ideas about "suitable jobs" for the handicapped ever hedged me in with prejudices. I was fortunate that I was never tantalized with warnings that there were vocational fields in which my handicap made me ineligible. Nobody has to point out to a crippled person the things he can and can't do. I certainly didn't aspire for a spot in a dancing chorus, but I never felt any restrictions about choice of vocation either. I was allowed to follow my own bents.

Although some handicapped people must inevitably compromise with their ambitions, I firmly believe that, in general, they can at least approximate their objectives in the field of their natural choice. It may, of course, involve a shift in emphasis, and they should be prepared for occasional rebuffs. Although I suffered few of these, I was unprepared for them.

An acquaintance of mine, a girl victimized by polio in her teens, has been committed to a wheel chair for life. When she began protesting the completely unproductive existence she was forced to endure, her family humored her in great style. They allowed her to become the unhappy pawn of a spinster cousin of her mother's who fancied herself an able amateur occupational therapist. This well-meaning relative kept the poor girl bored but busy making pot holders, stringing beads into hideous novelties, and weaving baskets. Only when my friend finally revolted against her helpful advisors did she achieve the independence she craved.

"I simply wasn't meant to be a bead stringer," she told me. She loved books and had planned, before tragedy touched her, to major in library science at Simmons College. With the assistance of a very small loan for working capital, she started a lending library in her own home. In addition, on her own initiative, she learned shorthand and typing. She ran a successful dual business—the library, and a public-stenography and notary-public service. It was not precisely the culmination of her original plans, but it was a close enough substitute to give her personal satisfaction, as well as economic independence.

I was unhindered by planted misgivings. With complete freedom of choice, I surveyed occupations for women—or rather, careers for women. (For what girl ever expects anything less than a career, complete with a fresh gardenia daily on a superbly tailored suit, and a big blond Philippine mahogany desk in which to keep her lipstick?)

I made my first trifling but unhesitating step into economic independence while I was still in college. For the munificent salary of thirty cents an hour, I did a few small chores around the campus. In addition to operating the dormitory switchboard and doing a little life-guarding of the girls' swimming pool, I also could be had as a baby sitter. Summers I guided the young, as a counselor in a girls' camp. For, absolutely free and with unrestrained rapture, I also worked every day on the college newspaper. I didn't actually contribute very heavily to my own support; I merely earned the money for a few frills.

But this brief prologue to economic realism jolted me into recognition of the elementary fact that a pay envelope was a nifty proposition, but getting it could be almighty dull. I decided to go into newspaper work which, I thought and still believe, wasn't the quick formula for riches but was certainly a fairly entertaining way to eke out an existence.

Those were the days when opportunity didn't knock, she walked right in and sat down cozylike in the kitchen and had a cup of coffee with you. All you had to do was tell her what you had in mind. But by 1930, when I actually had the sheepskin in my fist, Opportunity, the fickle wench, was off on a long vacation. When I finally went out to work my wiles on employers, the depression was on.

Although I still regarded life as a bowl of cherries, I knew the horrible truth: cherries had pits in them that sometimes broke the teeth. All I wanted was enough money to pay the dentist's bill. Any job was a good job. It's true, I never desperately got down to contemplating taking a blind partner and sitting on the sidewalk with a couple of tin cups, the last stand of the handicapped. But I did spend some time listing all the occupations that didn't require ten toes. There were lots of them and they all looked mighty entrancing to me. However, with the luck of the one-legged, I landed on my foot—right smack on a newspaper.

CHAPTER VIII

The Game

But I didn't start job-hunting for six months after I got out of college for the incredible reason that I promptly pranced off to Europe with a money belt bulging with traveler's checks around my middle. How this came about is a complicated story. Even with the knowledge that I may endanger the morale of poor normal people, I must admit that my exceedingly memorable junket was a direct reward for being one-legged. I went to Europe because I used crutches and because, about seven years prior to my date of sailing, when I was fourteen, our car broke down.

In a tempestuous tantrum, I was made to cross town on a trolley with Mother. We had an appointment to dine in formal splendor with a stiff relative who wore a little black band around her neck to restrain her excess chinnage. The prospect didn't send me into rapturous ecstasy. On such feeble threads hung one of the most important events of my life.

The trolley was crowded. I sat in a glum pout on

the open platform and Mother sat inside, glaring at me. Another trolley rider, who also proved to be a refugee from a temperamental automobile, pushed himself through the mob and hung onto a strap directly in front of Mother. When a seat became vacant next to her, he took it. Finally, with a good deal of diffidence, he opened fire.

"Is the little girl on crutches your daughter?" he whispered quietly.

He didn't quite fit the role, but Mother too promptly tagged him. He was, she assumed, an artificial-leg salesman. They frequently nailed her in public places when she was unwise enough to be seen with me. Their approach, however, usually had a certain slither to it. You almost expected them to whip out a card with an address on it and breathe in your ear, "Slip around some night, knock three times, and ask for Joe."

With understandable reluctance, considering how brattishly I was behaving at the moment, Mother confessed her maternity. She didn't warm up to the stranger. In spite of his charm, for he had a lot of it, Mother resisted him. When she discovered he wasn't a salesman, I think her next assumption was that he was a fugitive from an insane asylum for he said to her, "Your daughter charms me." Such a mad sentiment, reasonably enough, made Mother wary. And then he continued, "I wonder if you would be willing to allow my wife and me to call and get acquainted with her? We are very much interested in girls who use crutches."

Mother was not one to pass out our phone number promiscuously. Although she insisted later that she trusted the gentleman on sight, she made no exception in his case. She gave him a polite quick freeze, intended to make Birds Eye spinach out of him. I marvel that the poor man ever thawed sufficiently to do his detective work.

But he evidently had a sharp Sherlock mind and a couple of handy Watsons. In a mere matter of three days, anyway, an impeccable professional colleague of Father's telephoned and said that a very dear old friend of his was eager to meet our family. He brought him around to Father's office. It was Mama's "insane leg salesman." He turned out to be a prominent and highly esteemed Los Angeles professional man, the president of the Harvard Club, the president of the University Club, and a good Episcopalian—the latter being godly enough convoy to satisfy even Mother. He was also, I am personally convinced, the most thoroughly kind and gentle man who ever lived. Moreover, he and his equally lovable wife—strange as it seemed at the time—were minor collectors of one-legged girls. I say "minor" because I have since encountered several curators of much vaster collections of such curiosa. This collecting may sound like a form of madness—but if it is, the quite harmless syndrome invariably afflicts exceedingly nice people.

Mr. and Mrs. Fultz were a childless couple who first became interested in one-legged girls when one such served them very efficiently as a private secretary. Also they were influenced by a charming little tale published in book form in 1912, called *The Girl with the Rosewood Crutches.* This was a touching first-person account, anonymously signed, of a young woman's triumphant victory over the handicap of a right leg amputation. She was properly modest about herself, of course, since she was a perfect lady. Nevertheless, she didn't let the fact escape her readers for a moment that she was just about the most tantalizingly beautiful, and at the same time chaste, package that ever titillated a susceptible male. She walked like a queen, dressed like Mrs. Harrison Williams, sang like head bird at the Met, and had a brilliant career, as well as a devoted lover whom she coyly referred to as "The Boy."

My new friends gave me the book to read, and I too was greatly impressed by the romantic girl's autobiography. I even decided that if I ever got a sweetheart, I would call him "The Boy." I yearned to meet the author, even though I knew that time was afleeting and she was probably now a faded, doddering old crone of at least thirty.

Several years later, by one of those coincidences

that make life so entertaining for a person on crutches, I did meet "her." The book proved to be the bastard brain child of a big and bouncing and very jolly New York businessman and writer. He does use crutches, having a pair of unreliable knees, and he also possesses one of the country's most impressive collections of unipeds. But he is definitely not a fascinating little feminine hopper. Although he admits openly to a new legitimate book every year or so, he never confesses his paternity to *The Girl with the Rosewood Crutches*, that poor love child of his careless youth.

I don't know the chemistry of rapport. But whatever the element is that prompts strangers to recognize kinship with each other, it was bubbling to the point of bursting its beaker when I met Mr. and Mrs. Fultz. I loved them immediately—and more remarkable, they loved me. They became almost an extra pair of parents to me.

So to roam back to my original premise, because I used crutches and because Father's ancient Buick balked at precisely the right time, a couple of angels on lend-lease to the Earth gave me a trip to Europe for a graduation present.

This was a trifling contribution to my happiness, however, compared to the priceless one—the subtle contribution of influencing my attitude of mind—that they handed me on the installment plan over the years. Mr. Fultz gave me a healthy transfusion of his own rich imagination. He taught me how to use my crutches as tools for having a perfectly hell-raising good time.

He began, mildly enough, by attempting to put some artistry into my crutches. He presented me with my first pair of stylish sticks—beautiful rosewoods on which I strutted forth to claim my high school diploma. Prior to that I hadn't given anything but the most practical consideration to what sort of crutches I wore. I wanted them lightweight for ease in handling, and strong because I frequently broke them. I didn't care what they looked like. I even let my friends carve their initials all over them.

I was very cautious about the rubber tips worn on the ends, however. There are a great variety of these available, and I learned that the bigger and bulkier they were and the redder the rubber that went into them, the better. I always had spares on hand so that I could replace them promptly when one wore out. A crutch end protruding through a worn-out rubber tip is as dangerous as a planted banana peel on the sidewalk, and works precisely the same havoc. Giving up the big red suction-bottom safety crutch tips, and using substitute black synthetic ones, constituted the greatest commodity sacrifice I was called upon to make for the war effort. I'd rather have a car with no tires than crutches with inferior tips.

Mr. Fultz didn't settle back satisfied after giving

me the rosewood crutches. He turned out to have a hidden talent. He became a sort of Adrian to the Handicapped. It occurred to him, like an inspiration, that crutches should be regarded as smart accessories to a costume. He suggested that with my chocolate-colored rosewoods, I should wear a brown suède pump, purse, and gloves, and a brown felt hat. That was all the guidance I needed. In a few years, I had a crutch wardrobe: black, blue, brown, green, etc. Crutches don't come in gay colors but any good enamel works the enhancing transformation. I am now just as likely to complain, "I haven't got a crutch I'd wear to a dog fight," as I am to say, "I haven't got a decent dress to my name."

Others beside Mr. Fultz made contributions to the chic individuality of my crutch wardrobe, but it was he who first made me style-conscious. I have never possessed a really close friend who didn't take a tremendous critical interest in my crutches.

The "Father" of *The Girl with the Rosewood Crutches* gave me a very spritely pair of red ones. My brother-in-law, an engineer, really put some science into his improvement of my walking gear. He designed, cast saddle and handle connectives, and made me some beautiful slender crutches out of hollow Duralumin tubing. This material is magnificently suitable since it is light and very strong, and takes a neat baked enamel finish. These custom-built

Duralumins are now my prime favorites for dress crutches. They have the virtue of almost perpetual life; they don't get creaky with age; and they can be sent off for a new bake job to eradicate the ravages of rough use or to comply with current color schemes. Once, I even had a gilt-colored pair to match my gold evening slippers.

Another friend designed crutch cases for me. He had them custom-made to match my luggage. I can now conveniently carry two extra pairs along when I travel. These crutch carriers resemble gun cases and frequently on trains people ask me if I'm going hunting. I always say, "Yes, I'm a big-game hunter and have a den at home that is absolutely haunted with glassy-eyed heads."

Mr. Fultz's ideas, however, were not only aesthetic and practical, but lighthearted. Ingeniously, he carved out a little secret cache cabinet under the saddle of one of my wooden crutches. He said, "This will come in handy if you decide to be a diamond smuggler when you grow up, or an international spy who has to conceal the plan for the bomb sight." In the meantime, while I was still treading the paths of virtue, he suggested that I could always carry a dollar bill in it for mad money.

He, probably more than anyone I ever knew, embedded the conviction in my mind that there was nothing I couldn't do on crutches. He even whipped out *Webster* and gave me a consoling definition for handicap; "Handicap: A race or contest in which, in order to equalize chances of winning, an artificial disadvantage is imposed on a superior contestant." To prove *Webster's* point, he promptly set about disproving any limitation I admitted.

He taught me to drive a car, dance on one crutch, and how to master surf swimming. Many were the dollars he invested in encouraging my passion for horseback riding. More deviously, he infused into my consciousness recognition of my unique personal opportunity for adventure in living. He almost had me sorry for two-leggers.

Probably his greatest single inspiration in the gay spirit was the question and answer game which he dubbed "Ham and Legs." This is an entertaining indoor and outdoor sport from which ordinary people are barred because of the handicap of their normalcy. Occasionally friends of mine have opportunity to indulge in the game but only in the role of middleman.

Everyone who has walked on crutches knows thoroughly the great streak of curiosity that seems to be part and parcel of the American character. From the time I hobbled forth on my first pair of crutches at eight, right up to yesterday, perfect strangers not only have stared at me as if I were a bearded lady from the circus, but they have stopped me on the street, nailed me down in railroad cars, accosted me in stations and stores, and questioned me.

I have become very adept at recognizing the precise type of individual who will pose this $64 question, "My poor young lady, whatever happened to you?" In my mature dignity—such as it is—I have also developed a frigid unapproachable mien with which, when I choose to, I can freeze the question unasked in almost any throat.

But for many years, while I was younger and more defenseless, I could scarcely walk a city block without having someone pounce upon me and demand all the bloody details of my accident from the moment of collision right up to the fee extracted by my surgeon. This used to cause me acute embarrassment. I didn't have the necessary defiance to say, "It's none of your damn business." Besides, Mother didn't allow me to swear. I always paused and politely related my unimpressive little bicycle-meets-automobile fray.

It was Mr. Fultz who conceived of putting drama into this situation. Drama was, in fact, the essence of the game. I always had a mildly wistful regret that I couldn't take up acting, at least as a hobby. However there are few roles that are suitable for a one-legged Thespian—Sarah Bernhardt's advanced years on the stage as a uniped notwithstanding.

"This is your chance to do a little acting," Mr. Fultz told me. "Moreover you won't have to run through all the minor maid's roles before getting a chance to star. You can play the lead every time. You see, these people aren't really interested in you personally. They are merely starved for excitement. They pry, in the hope of uncovering a lurid hair-raising tale. I'm sure most of them are pretty well blasted by the commonplace truth. So, why not hand them precisely what they want? They're asking for it."

The game, Ham and Legs, provided all the answers. For a couple of evenings Mr. and Mrs. Fultz and I went into hysterics planning my attacks.

In the beginning I wasn't very adroit. I felt a soap-in-the-mouth guilt the first time I explained to a nosy old bat that I was the unfortunate offspring of a circus clown and a lion tamer and that I lost my leg by falling off a high tightrope where as a child I habitually played with my dolls.

Like most sinners, of course, I eventually became quite cavalier about my personal wickedness. The Ham came juicier and juicier with the Legs. Even the dizziest legends didn't give me the mildest prick of conscience. I suffered not a qualm but only the greatest pleasure from my premeditated prevarication.

There is apparently only one trait in human nature which is stronger than curiosity. It is credulity. The things people will believe are unbelievable!

One of my choicest little epics was the heroic account of a swooping venture on skis. Down a precipitous mountainside I *slalomed,* a sick baby in my arms, only to collapse at the doctor's door, the infant saved, but my poor right leg frozen stiff as a poker. It was so completely refrigerated, in fact, that the doctor, without administering so much as a whiff of anesthetic, chipped it off with an ice pick.

Even unrehearsed repartee came easily. The flapping-eared recipient of the latter fancy cheerfully swallowed the hook, and was all agape for the line and sinker. How did it happen that my left leg was so providentially spared, she wanted to know, not satisfied with what I already regarded as a very generous slice of my imagination.

"Well, I've been educated about weather," I said. "Me, I'm a Norska from Oslo. I was smart enough to anticipate chilblains. I decided I'd preserve at least one leg. Owed it to myself, I figured. I skied on only one foot, after pinning up my spare in a blanket."

"Well, I do declare!" The hypnotized listener didn't bat an eyelash.

In this little intellectual sport one has to carefully evaluate the proponents and the circumstances of play. For instance, the above choice item is best peddled in a sunny clime, where a general ignorance about skiing prevails. I recommend it as highly suitable to Los Angeles, California, but not quite so effective in Hanover, New Hampshire. It's fairly good training in psychology to estimate at a glance just how tall a tale each individual sucker will reach for. In general, the vocally inquisitive aren't mental giants. Sometimes, however, I have to content myself with something simple like leprosy or an encounter with an ill-mannered shark off the coast of Florida.

There is another important complication to the game with special laws of honor. Mr. Fultz was a very kindly man and he wrote these specifications into the rule book at the very beginning. An ethical player must distinguish between the idly inquisitive who deserve to have their ears pinned back and the genuinely interested who frequently have a heartfelt reason for inquiry. Often I am approached by some-one who has a similarly handicapped member in his family. Strangely enough, these querists are a breed apart. They look different and their approach is much gentler. There is a certain softness of eye in contrast to the glittering rapaciousness of the sensation-seeker's leer.

"I hope you'll forgive me for speaking to you, but I have a son—" That is almost a standard opener for these questioners.

Then the game is no longer Ham. "Let's sit down some place where we can talk," I suggest. In ex-change for my own genuine but rather mundane autobiography, I hear someone else's story. Frequently these are heroic histories that make me apologetic for the happy simplicity of my own life.

Of course, the game is dangerous if played too close to home. My legends occasionally fly back to nest in my hair.

According to a rumor that I have reason to credit, the world's a small place. Even in New York City, where the chances are you'll never meet your next-door neighbor socially even if you flit from party to party for a lifetime, I had one of my stories return and lay a double-yolked egg on me.

In a beauty salon where I sat under a noisy drier, a similarly trapped customer next to me, apparently obsessed with her curiosity, screamed, "What happened to you?" Anyone who is nosy in a high cackle deserves the chopping block.

"Parachutist!" I yelled back. "Stunt flyer!" I threw up my hands as if the very thought of the horrible details pained me beyond further speech.

She passed a frail white manicured hand across her cheek, elevated her bosom in a sympathetic sigh, and shook her hot head. That was the extent of our girlish confidences.

Three days later I went to a cocktail party in the apartment of a close friend. I believe there are some eight million people in New York City. Only about fifteen of them were at the party, but—all fancy with her new permanent—there was Milady of the Drier. I probably wouldn't even have recognized her except that when I came tripping in on my crutches, I heard her gasp to our hostess, "Elaine, darling, you never told me you knew that perfectly fascinating parachutist."

Elaine who immediately recognized one of my wayward flights of fancy gave me a cynical diabolical smile. "Oh, didn't I tell you—dear?" answered Elaine. "Sad, wasn't it? And losing her teeth, too." She paused to click her tongue sympathetically. "Did she tell you about that? I think the dentist did a rather neat job on her double dentures though. But you should see her when they're out. Is she a sight!" There was nothing I could do at that point but show my allegedly false biters in a horrible smile.

The only questioners who really ruffle me are children. "Mama, where's that lady's leg?" Junior invariably points his finger at me. Very promptly, and as firmly as if he'd just taken the name of the Lord in vain, he is silenced by Mama.

Sometimes the child asks me directly, however. "Where's your leg, lady?"

Then I'm almost as tongue-tied and twice as embarrassed as a young thing out on her first date. Usually I say, "It's all gone," and run like hell. If the dear little inquiring mind belongs to a child old enough to digest a good moral tale, I often pause and deliver. With that hearty cheerfulness that is so unbecoming to an adult talking to the very young, I croak, "When I was a little girl like you, I didn't mind my mother when she told me I mustn't play in the street and I got very badly hurt."

"A car hit you and your leg broke off, huh?" Children brought up on the bloody adventures of current so-called "comics" can take a mere loss of leg with unflinching calm. But I can't hand it out with similar detachment.

"That's right," I agree and hotfoot it for cover.

I like my adversaries to be of voting age. Then they get no quarter. In this game there are some very special gambits. My favorite is the death-dealing Fool's Mate. This is only applicable when some hopelessly snoopy old biddy is stupid enough to leave herself wide open."

"My poor girl, I see you've lost your leg."

That's the opportunity for the *touche*, "How careless of me!"

CHAPTER IX

"Watch Your Step"

I DON'T want to imply that I harbor the cheerful notion that being one-legged is a privilege. It's a damn nuisance, of course. Whether on an artificial leg or on crutches, it always involves the constant annoying necessity of draying something along in the way of special walking gear. It is much handier to be equipped with standard attachments. Still, there is nothing that so convincingly argues for the Law of Compensation as traveling on crutches. Before I hied myself off to Europe, I wasn't a seasoned vagabond, by any means, but I had timidly taken a few Pullman rides to various parts of the country. I learned from experience that nobody got more for his money in service, consideration, and entertainment than I did. And when I set forth alone for my grand tour of the United States and the Continent, I had no haunting fear that I wouldn't get along fine.

Both passengers and railroad personnel always hover over me like guardian angels. It is true that occasionally over-solicitude upsets me—sometimes literally.

Pullman porters, a noble breed of men, in their kind eagerness to get me off the cars and off their hands without casualty, are likely to uncrutch me. When they have the cooperation of a conductor in unloading me—a doubly effective team—they can really work havoc. One on each side, grabbing my arm or my crutch, they frequently unbalance me. I am always safer managing steps or stairs of any kind without assistance. It is disheartening to blast their generosity by ordering them to unhand me. People simply glow with pleasure when they help the handicapped, and I have a theory that it is only decent to let them have their silly fun. So if I think the chances of survival, without broken bones, are about fifty-fifty, I take the gamble and endure the assistance, merely out of politeness.

Once, however, with two of the goodwill boys helpfully heckling me, I quite involuntarily took off from the top step of a Pullman car. By good fortune, plus what I modestly fancy was miraculous agility, I flew through the air with the greatest of ease and made a perfect three-point landing—one foot, two crutches. Even though breathless over my own accomplishment, I was able to pull myself together sufficiently to pass out quite an impressive bon mot. I turned to my horrified helpers and said nonchalantly, "Don't worry—I always get off that way."

Another thorn in my flesh, who sports a heart of

gold, is the over-zealous redcap who spots me invariably as I am being knocked off the train by a porter. He dashes off like a breeze to get me a wheel chair. He then offers to convey me right through the station out to the cab stand. Of course, I don't want or need a wheel chair, and even urged on by my obliging nature, I can't bring myself to crawl into one.

On only one occasion did I ever succumb to a redcap with the standard equipage. This occurred during the first stage of my trip to Europe on my stopover between trains in Chicago. This hero to whom I fell prey had a most appealing, smiling, shiny black face under his white hair. In spite of the retarded gait of his advanced years, he pulled up promptly with his proffered transportation. He was so obviously pleased with himself and so genuinely solicitous of me that I couldn't flip off his beaming light by refusing to ride. With resignation and a great show of clumsiness, I got myself into the wheel chair, with both the train porter and the redcap behaving like derricks. I paid an extra dollar in tips for my embarrassment and the drayage I didn't want.

"You just sit back now and relax," the good Samaritan cooed at me on the way to the passengers' gate. "You're gonna get along just mighty fine. Is somebody gonna meet you, Honey?"

Somebody was gonna meet her, Honey admitted with some disquietude. My aunt was right there behind the gate. She saw me as I approached in my stylish chaise and grabbed at the iron grill work as if she were about to rip it out by its tap roots. She visibly paled.

"Oh, my dear! My dear! You've had an accident!" she gasped. "What happened to you?"

"There, there, Auntie," I soothed as I rolled my eyes roguishly in an effort to let her in on my harmless ruse. "It's really all right. I've just lost my leg, that's all. But I'm going to get along just fine."

Auntie, dear soul, was not tuned in to catch the most blatant innuendoes that morning. "Heavenly Father!" she screeched for all Chicago to hear. "Lost the other one?"

I kicked up my fine, genuine old ancestral foot, to relieve her mind, but she still looked ready to take off.

"Now, don't you go grieving this young lady," the nice old redcap reproved. "She's only got one foot and I expect it would'a been better if she'd told you when it happened so it wouldn't'a been such a shock to you, but you'll only upset her if you carry on like this. God moves in mysterious ways." The old boy was quite a philosophical gentleman. Of course, poor, mystified Auntie had been notified promptly enough of my loss thirteen years before.

"As soon as we get in your car, I'll tell you all about it, Auntie." I twisted my mouth into a horrible grimace, winked my eye broadly, and shook my head. Apparently the combination of contortions finally made some sense—or rather nonsense, from Auntie's point of view.

"Oh, you are simply *terrible,*" she announced in her relief. "You ought to be ashamed of yourself. You always were a difficult child."

If Auntie had taken a good look at the redcap at that precise moment, she would, I am sure, have fled in fright. He had her death warrant plainly written on his face. Her lack of feeling even shocked the philosophy right out of the dear old man.

I can imagine him sitting among his fellow burden-bearers. "You sure run into all kinds in this game," he probably begins. "But the queerest character I ever saw—barring none—" And then, I bet Auntie gets a good going over.

My visit with Auntie was off to a bad start. During my four-hour layover in Chicago, she wouldn't even give me a peaceful country-girl's gawk at Marshall Field's finery. She spent the entire time lecturing me on how a lady conducted herself on a tour.

With horrible detail she covered the subjects of the insidious evils of strong drink, cardsharpers on ship-board, and the general depravity of the human race. Her final admonition as she put me on the Capitol Limited for Washington, where I was going to get a glimpse of the Government, was, "Now watch your step. Don't ever speak to a stranger—especially a man." I believe she expected me to spend the next six months in dead silence.

I had a charming male friend staked out in the club car, however, before we got to the Englewood station. Only by crass discourtesy or by investing in a compartment and never leaving it, even for a breath of air or breakfast, can a crippled traveler keep himself aloof. My friend was a gentleman who came under the category of honorable opponent in the Ham and Legs game. He was a United States attorney and he had a friend, a Senator, whose little boy had just suffered an accident which necessitated the amputation of his leg. I always figure that only the most respectable people have handicapped friends or family. Besides, few individuals ever plan to do wrong to a poor little Nell who so obviously has already had plenty of wrong done her. Crutches are a great protection.

When he invited me to dinner in the diner, I hesitated only long enough to tell him about my quaint aunt. "She told me just before we pulled out of the station not to take up with strange men. But my aunt is very naïve. She hasn't been around much."

"And you, my dear young lady, are very sophisticated, I can see that," he answered. "You look as if you'd just been 'round and 'round."

This put me in a genial mood. I even smoked a

cigarette to prove to him that his confidence in my worldliness was not misplaced. We had a fine dinner. The next morning when I got off the train in Washington, however, my friend apparently had had a change of heart about my sophistication.

"I don't think you should run around this strange city alone," he said. He carefully arranged my sightseeing, lunched me at the Cosmos Club, and personally stowed me on the Philadelphia train in the afternoon. Moreover, he gave me a stack of his personal cards on which he had carefully written out for me an introduction to somebody woefully respectable in almost every capital of Europe and one for the captain of the *Leviathan,* the ship on which I was to sail. "You may not need these," he said, "but it will make me easier in my mind for you to have them. Now watch your step and don't take up with strangers."

He blasted my faith. He might just as well have been a blood-brother to Auntie.

On the train to Philadelphia, I picked up with another interesting, kind stranger. He was from an entirely different social level from my Washington protector. He was a former taxi driver from Brooklyn. He had been forced to give up his career when he suffered an accident in which he lost his left arm. He wore a hook. He was very cheerful about his fate, however, since he had become a traveling salesman which he regarded as a good leap up the ladder. He told me to call him "Elmer." We had a dandy time confiding the stories of our lives to each other. He had a wife whom he referred to as "Maze"—short for Maizie, I suppose—and seven children all devoutly named for saints. He told me exactly how to have a big time in "Philly."

When we arrived he helped me locate my uncle in the Philadelphia station. Whenever possible, my family had carefully posted a relative where I was scheduled to light. Proudly I introduced Elmer to my uncle who displayed a certain cold restraint. When the father of the seven saints offered to take us to a nice little speak-easy near by, Uncle became actively antagonistic and spirited me away. I waved back, however, and called "Good-by, Elmer."

My understanding friend lifted his hook in a jovial gesture, yelled "Olive oil, Louise," and implied by a genial wink that he knew what I was in for—and no hard feelings. Uncle shuddered like a victim of the shakes.

Then began two days of lectures. Uncle was very broad minded and sensibly tolerant. He admitted readily enough that I couldn't seal my lips with adhesive for six months. He assured me, in fact, that it was perfectly all right to speak to strangers on trains and boats. But, he firmly pointed out, I must watch for symbols of respectability in men. I might fraternize, to the cozy extent of discussing the weather, with the following, listed in preferred order: gentlemen of the clergy whom I could identify by their collars, Kiwanians whose identity he made plain by displaying his own lapel button, and Masons. Generally speaking, he distrusted women, especially those traveling alone. A bad lot! He confessed, however, that it might be safe to converse with nuns.

"Oh, Boy, Unc!" I chirped happily. "Am I going to have myself a time!"

He let me have a gander at the Liberty Bell and bought me some excellent seafood fodder in a place called Bookbinder's, which has nothing to do with the publishing business but means *restaurant* in "Philadelphian." The rest of the time, he showed me around socially among some worthy citizens of Chestnut Hill who clucked at me over their lovely china teacups and assured me I was a fine, brave girl to flit about all by myself on my crutches on treacherous trains and ships and such like. They, too, knew the chorus to the old refrain, "But watch your step!" Uncle and his friends, I suspect, had lived too long in close proximity to the Liberty Bell. At least, it struck me that they bore one delicate stamp of similarity—just the tiniest touch of crack.

I had a good, wholesome time in Philadelphia—which led me to the conclusion that I'd contrive cleverly to avoid the New York family contingent. Relatives were so overstimulating. I was afraid I'd give up the whole trip and hunt up a good lively Sunday School picnic as a substitute if I were exposed to any more of my righteous kin. I was supposed to wire a cousin in Rye of my train schedule from Philadelphia. He had promised Mother to come down to Manhattan to meet me and then watch over me like a fond father until I sailed four days later. I hadn't seen this hazy sprig on the family tree in some fifteen years and, understandably, my memory of him was blurred.

So I only pretended to wire him. Uncle put me on the train, with one last warning that rang a strangely nostalgic note: "Watch your step now." He was cheerfully relieved to be disposed of me, I suspect. Triumphantly I took over New York all by myself.

I discovered later on, however, that the one relative I avoided so assiduously was a very smooth and handsome piece of goods who must have gotten into the family under false pretenses or by some miscarriage of cargo on the part of a careless stork. He tracked me down before I sailed, sent me a brace of orchids, and the only admonition he administered was in the form of a neat little list of French and German wines which he commissioned me, with a fifty-dollar bill, to taste in his honor.

"Won't I get drunk?" I asked with breathless awe.

"Not on fifty dollars spread around," he assured me. "And what if you do? If you stagger, everyone will just say, 'Look at that poor cripple, what a hard time she has walking on those crutches.' My God!" he chortled, warming to the thought. "What a handy alibi they'd make."

He was such a nice man.

CHAPTER X

All at Sea

WHEN I boarded the *Leviathan,* there wasn't a soul to see me off. I got to pondering on this woeful situation while I watched the abandon with which almost everyone else was being kissed. I turned my morbid imagination to California, where I pictured every woman under fifty who was still sound of limb, panting with eagerness to snatch my man while my back was turned. After all, he hadn't gotten around to making me an honorable proposal. One dire thought marched along behind another dire thought like a funeral procession. I brooded over the discouraging fact that I was on only a temporary reprieve from unemployment. I got frantic trying to remember how much I was supposed to tip the deck steward. I was certain I was going to be seasick—in fact, my stomach was already turning cart wheels. I speculated on the chances of a repetition of the *Titanic* disaster. I tried to recollect the words of "Nearer My God to Thee" and could only plug the parody "Nero My Dog Has Fleas." This, I knew, would never be appropriate during that moment which I now regarded as inevitable—when I went down with the ship after giving my place in the lifeboat to a pregnant mother. I even entertained a couple of terrified reflections on Auntie's predictions about Mickey Finns and cardsharpers. I yearned for a clergyman, a Kiwanian, or a Mason to drop by and mention the weather. I was in a state completely out of the Union.

To escape the tantalizing view of people mauling each other, I went into the deserted lounge and sat down and cried and cried in the most dejected misery. An impartial observer might very well have assumed that I had just been chained to first oar on a slave galley.

"You want something to cry in, young lady? No beer—how about a coke?" It was a steward. "Your family making you go abroad because you been raising hell? You in trouble, I betcha, huh?"

It should have cheered me that someone thought I looked dangerous enough to have been raising hell, but it didn't. The sentiment only added to my misery. "No," I sobbed on. "Darn it, I'm not the type that gets into trouble."

"Oh, you're not that bad," he consoled. "I betcha you'll be in real swell trouble before we dock at Southampton. Drink up." He shoved a Coca-Cola at me.

I fumbled for my purse.

"This is unofficial," he shook his head. "On the house. Now pull yourself together and go out on deck. We're about to get under way and you don't want to miss that."

I sniffled, blew my nose and repaired the awful red thing with powder. I got up and tucked my crutches under my arms, still feeling very sympathetic with myself.

"Look sharp for the coaming when you go out—watch your step." If he'd been a practicing psychiatrist who'd had me laid out on a couch for six months boring into my inhibitions, he couldn't have hit more inspired therapeutics.

I quit handing myself condolences. It threw me right into a laughing fit.

He looked uneasy. "Was that good or something?"

"Oh, very good," I said, "even though I have heard it before. It's just an old family joke that gets funnier and funnier. I'm going to be fine now. Thanks."

"I'll keep an eye on you this trip."

"Swell—you watch my step for me."

He did, too. I never sat down in the lounge for a drink or an innocent game of bridge that he didn't slink up, squint his brows suspiciously, and scrutinize carefully whatever man I'd managed to snag. It was a little disconcerting to me, and it definitely made my victims uneasy. One sterling Cornell boy, in fact, protested. "That steward is certainly a queer duck—and damned rude if you ask me. The way he goes over me, you'd think I'd just held up the purser. If he dared lay his hands on me, I think he'd frisk me."

As I walked out on deck, I thought I'd suddenly gone to Heaven and was tuned in on a choir of angels. The orchestra was playing "Our Sturdy Golden Bear." Californians in the crowd, even boys from Stanford who don't go for that tune, were all lit up proudly as if each one of them had personally planted every orange tree in the Golden State. The orchestra was a bunch of boys from the University of California who were playing their way to Europe. I, too, showed my good California ivories in a broad smile. As the ship weighed anchor, all the West Coasters were shaking hands and banging each other on the back. From a lonely wake, I suddenly leaped into Wednesday of old home week.

Not at all surprising to a person on crutches, some of these native sons and daughters even recognized me. "Aren't you from Los Angeles? I am sure I remember seeing you shopping in Bullocks." Of course, they didn't actually remember me—they remembered my identifying crutches. Crutches, a sure tag, discourage a one-legger from a life of crime, but they are likely to be profitable in any situation short of bank robbery. And even then I'm pretty sure they'd soften up a jury almost as much as a hunk of tasty cheesecake. Certainly they gave me a good start socially on shipboard.

A bouncing, bright-faced man tapped me on the arm and said, "How'd you like that chocolate soda you had Friday in Schrafft's?" I looked at him in astonishment.

"I was sitting right there beside you at the counter," he said. "I had vanilla."

He was the social director of the *Leviathan* and he regarded our former encounter as an occult sign. He made me his protégée. Every night he lifted the rope and let me and several selected friends in on the sacred revelry in first cabin. This was a dubious privilege since the passengers in Third while less heavily laden with lucre were much lighter on their feet. It was also comforting to hear "Our Sturdy Golden Bear" every night, even though Ben Bernie's music in First was perhaps eight beats to the bar more professional.

It is a curious eccentricity, but people have a tendency to regard girls on crutches as a special breed who behave—or should behave, anyway—entirely differently from other humans. During one crossing I had a charming old lady as my cabin mate. She was very much concerned about my welfare. In fact, I think it was her main interest in life, since she didn't approve of much of anything that went on aboard ship.

I was much more agile than she, but I practically had to knock her senseless to get her to take the lower berth. She was solicitous of my metabolism and always inquired daily about my diet and elimination. "You can't be too careful on crutches," she told me solemnly. "You must keep up your strength." What she wanted me to keep it up for, I certainly can't imagine.

She had a disconcerting habit of sitting bolt upright in bed when I came in at night—checking the time by her watch. Then, apparently completely puzzled, she demanded, "Now, will you tell me please what a young lady on crutches does on shipboard until one o'clock in the morning?"

One time I was bold enough to make a little arch inquiry on my own. "What do you think young ladies without crutches do?" I asked her.

"Oh, mercy goodness!" she gasped. "You don't do *that,* do you?"

When I arrived in London from the boat train, I became the ward of a professional guide who took me and a varied bunch of recalcitrants in tow for a tour of the Shakespeare country. From then on, most of my traveling in Great Britain and on the Continent was done under the wing of some such bird. These couriers usually could chirp in several languages and they had apparently been good boys in their youth and read a chapter from Baedeker every night. There was little of historical, artistic or ecclesiastical value that I was allowed to escape. I was luckier than some, of course. I only had one aching foot instead of two.

My first realization that I was marked for special enchantment far beyond that afforded by the British Museum and the Louvre came on the way to Warwick. We all spewed out of our sight-seeing bus in a small village and everyone scattered for an hour of freedom. I went into a little shop that specialized in charming, overpriced bric-a-brac. A very pleasant-looking man, obviously the proprietor, gave my every move in his establishment rapt, exclusive attention, to the great neglect of all his other customers.

I even got the rather disquieting notion that he suspected me of being a shoplifter. Finally, in my embarrassment, with a false show of haughtiness, I started to leave. When I reached the door, he called to me.

"Young lady—please—just a moment." He was obviously perturbed about something.

"There is an item, rather choice," he spoke in a low voice, "that I keep in the back room. I would like to show it to you."

Fascinated by his strange behavior and the sudden conviction that it wasn't a shoplifter he fancied me but a countess, incognito, out bargaining for jewels, I followed him. If his appearance hadn't been so consolingly respectable, I am sure I would have worried when he brushed his other customers out the door.

"I'm closing shop for half an hour," he announced curtly. "Please come back later." They were all so obviously annoyed, however, that I am certain none of them returned.

"Forgive my most discourteous behavior," he pleaded when we were alone. "You see, I have a little girl, just nine, who has a handicap similar to yours. She is only five weeks out of hospital. Would you—could you—"

"Oh, of course," I interrupted him. "I would be delighted to meet her. I was eight when I was hurt. Maybe I can tell her something useful."

He led me through a back door of the shop and into a little walled garden where a small pale child with a doll sat listlessly in a wheel chair. A young woman sat beside her with a book of fairy tales in her lap.

"Elizabeth," the shop proprietor said, "here is an American lady who has come to see Mary."

They gave me tea while I talked to the little girl. I walked up and down the garden on my crutches and even went in for a bit of fancy exhibitionism—holding up my one foot and using the crutches like stilts, a trick that always appeals to children. I passed on some of the things that I learned when I was just about the age of the little English girl. I quoted my old friend, Mrs. Ferris—even to recommending the multiplication tables. I told the little girl that life was going to be lots of fun for her. I am afraid it may not have proved so, but I believed what I said in 1930 and she believed me, too. When I left she laughed and waved her hand and assured me she would have her crutches and be ready to race me to the corner the next time I came through.

Her father ushered me through the shop where he paused long enough to take a delicately beautiful unset cameo from a velvet-lined tray. "From Mary," he said, and handed it to me. "Please take it," he urged, when I hesitated.

Excess generosity is one of the problems a handicapped person faces. I have found that I am more likely to err in refusing than accepting. Seats offered me in crowded cars; special consideration in the queue at a theater; porters rushing through trains to open doors for me; shoppers giving me their turn at a busy counter in a store—and even cameos, presented by strangers. They all pose a problem.

A handicapped person doesn't win any of these on his merit, and frequently he doesn't require any such thoughtfulness. In my childhood and teens, I am sure I was very rude in my constant huffy refusals of any kind of aid. I have grown more mellow, more sensible, and, I believe, more kindly.

Frequently I accept proffered places in crowded buses or trolleys, from tired, elderly men who I know need the seats much more than I. But, according to faultless authority, "It is more blessed to give than to receive." For the most part, I am convinced it is up to the handicapped person graciously to let the giver be blessed.

I took the lovely little cameo, and I sincerely believe that the Englishman was just as happy over the gift as I was.

CHAPTER XI

In No Sense a Broad

In Holland my crutches introduced me into another family circle. This time, a very old gentleman in Amsterdam started talking to me at a great rate in Dutch. Grandma, dear old cynic, had especially warned me against foreigners.

"Don't believe a word they say. You mustn't trust a man who can't speak English. You never know what nonsense he may be handing you."

It is true, I didn't know one word of Dutch, but I am sure even Grandmother would have understood the old gentleman. For one thing, he held his two hands folded together on his chest—a protuberance which blended and lost itself in a tremendous stomach —and he bobbed his head and smiled in a manner completely benign. As his conversation continued—or rather his monologue, for I didn't say anything except, "American, American"—he made gestures.

He pointed at my leg and then made a violent slashing motion at his own, and surprisingly enough for one of his age and bulk, he did a few deep-knee bends. I decided he must wear an artificial leg on which he was obviously an agile performer.

He grinned broadly, pointed into space and made a beckoning motion. "Speak English," he put in as a lure, but there was no doubt he was referring to someone else's talents. I followed him across the street and halfway down the block where he paused in front of an orthopedic supply shop.

The window displayed the usual obscenely naked legs, trusses, braces, crutches, bizarre corsets, etc. At the door we were met by a square, blond Hollander who wore a leather apron and who limped slightly. Here apparently was the artificial leg—not on the old man. The elderly gentleman still beaming contentedly, once more gave out a great mouthful of his own language.

The younger man then turned to me and spoke in excellent English. "This is my old father. He brought you here because he believes that in America they do not have the artificial legs. My father thinks only the Dutch are so smart." He laughed. "He wanted you to see the Dutch legs such as I wear. My father believes the Indians still fight the white people over the sea and that maybe you were shot with the poisoned arrow. He thinks I am the very important people because I make the legs."

"Well, I think you're very important, too," I agreed.

"I'd very much like to see your shop. Do you have your knee? You walk very well."

This is a question always of prime interest among artificial-leg wearers.

"No knee," he told me. "Do you have the knee?"

This conversation between strangers may seem somewhat off the polite path of small talk, but it is a typical opener between amputees.

The young Hollander took me into the back room and gave me a stool to sit on while he proudly demonstrated his machine tools by shaving the epidermis off a couple of half-finished thighs. His father got out some polish and carefully rubbed a shine on my rosewood crutches. As he worked he muttered, "Good, good, speak English, good, good," under his breath, smiling all the while in a way that would have satisfied even Grandmother.

The old man followed us around and once more began pouring out his Dutch. He raised his voice to a higher and higher pitch, apparently of the conviction that if he spoke loud enough I'd eventually understand him.

"My father wants to give you the beer or the chocolate," the younger man interpreted.

Again I was the cause of a shop closing at an odd hour. The three of us walked down the block to a confectionary where we imbibed a thick delicious chocolate drink.

The incident wasn't, I suppose, especially significant. I have seen many shops similar to the one in Amsterdam, and I had the price of a cup of chocolate in my purse. But during my European travels, stopping in the favorite tourist hotels and invading museums that had already thoroughly bored the local citizenry, I met only Americans. I like Americans. They're dandy, but they weren't exactly a novelty. I'd been running into them for years.

It was fun to meet the natives, a privilege that was mine merely because I didn't wear two shoes. The fact that the Hollanders behaved precisely like Americans put special meaning in the incident. It gave me evidence that there are no national boundaries to the appeal in a pair of crutches.

My prize experience, in which the crutches played the leading role, occurred in Paris. It was a very startling case of mistaken identity. I am frequently taken for some other one-legged girl. In Los Angeles, for instance, I have a friend, Ruth Wright, a very clever decorator, who also has a right leg amputation. I have been mistaken for her upon a number of occasions for no reason at all except that we both use crutches and frequent the same haunts. We don't resemble each other in the least. She has been mistaken for me, too. On several occasions acquaintances of mine have asked me, "Who was that distinguished-looking bearded man I saw you with the other night?" Ruth's husband is a distinguished gentleman with a beard, but I don't go out with him in the evenings.

I should have remembered this tendency to misidentify, that day in Paris, but it didn't occur to me. I was strolling along the Place de L'Opera one afternoon, decked out in my best navy and white print, my white hat and white crutches. I was happily minding my own negligible business which consisted in gawking at people and marveling at the continually amazing fact that I was in Paris strolling along the Place de L'Opera, in my best navy and white print, etc.

All of a sudden, I felt someone touch my arm. Startled, I turned to look into the serious face of a thin, bespectacled young man. He looked as if he'd been reared in a library and eaten the leaves from dictionaries in lieu of lettuce. Except for the fact that he seemed to be speaking fluent French, he might have been an academic genius from almost any American college.

"*Je ne voudrai que causer avec vous, mademoiselle,*" he said. "*Je vous payerai l'honoraire habituel. Je suis écrivain, vous voyez, et je vais écrire un livre dans lequel il y a un caractère comme vous.*"

His recitation seemed to cause him acute discomfort, but I didn't recognize his complaint from my avid study of a valuable volume entitled, BRIGHTER

French, *Colloquial, Idiomatic, and (mildly) Technical for* Bright Young People *(who already know some).* This was a splendid little collection of witty repartee, and although I learned a bright saying from it daily, I never seemed to choose one that came in handy.

The young man appeared to be suffering from something—frustrated love, I decided, or a bilious attack.

Being loath to admit my shocking ignorance, I said, "*Oui, oui,*" and pointed off vaguely in the opposite direction. Apparently this was a satisfactory reply.

"*Epatant!*" the young man said, and hung onto my arm like a leech. He seemed increasingly distressed about life.

"*Epatant,* your own self!" I shook myself free. "What's the matter with you anyway?"

I fell naturally into English since I couldn't fall naturally into anything else.

"My gosh!" he gasped and blushed to the roots of his blond hair which, incidentally, could have stood the services of a good barber. He pulled himself away from me as if I were a fallen woman who'd threatened his spotless celibacy. "You're an American girl!"

"What do I look like—Ethiopian?" I snapped. "You don't look so Latin yourself."

"Oh, I'm an American, certainly. And honestly I do beg your pardon. But, you know, really—let me tell you something. You shouldn't use those white crutches. My goodness, I should say you shouldn't—not in Paris!"

"I certainly don't know what concern it is of yours," I said primly, and stiffening my back I hastened off down the street. But he came plodding right along behind me.

"Honestly, I'm telling you—do what I say—" he gasped. "Don't use the white crutches. I'd say the same thing to my own sister."

"Well, you just run along then and tell your sister not to wear her white crutches."

"Oh, my sister doesn't use crutches. You see—"

"I see all right," I announced righteously. "You are intoxicated and if you don't let me alone I'll call a cop—I mean a *gendarme*."

In sheer desperation I got in a taxicab. Nothing was so distracting to me as trying to count the proper tip for a Paris cab driver. The dejected lad just stood on the sidewalk shaking his head sadly while I drove away.

I almost forgot this peculiar performance in the excitement of getting ready to go out that evening. I was invited to a very gay and very "Latin" party with Benny Tompkins, a dreamy-looking boy with a beard from Brooklyn. That is, Benny was from Brooklyn. The beard was pure Parisian. He was in Paris studying art. He was cleverly learning to paint familiar things so they couldn't be recognized. I imagine he came in mighty handy in camouflage during the war.

I dressed myself up all fancy, including a horrible pair of dangling, bizarre earrings. It struck me pleasantly that I looked exactly like an exotic temptress. I was very elated over this pending festivity since it was going to be just terribly "Frenchy." As a matter of fact, there wasn't anything there more French than a four-year major in the subject from Harvard, U.S.A. Still, it satisfied me. I felt that I was living dangerously —part of the fast International Set. We sat on the floor in a dank apartment and drank wine, and the girls didn't look quite nice to me. However, when I recall my own getup for the occasion, I suspect we all looked about the same.

Shortly after I got there, in came the woeful-faced complainer with the white-crutch complex.

"My goodness!" I whispered to Benny, "that man who just came in is crazy."

"He's nuts all right," Benny agreed. "He's trying to write a book that is just chock-full of sin and I don't think he's ever done anything more daring in his life than get intimate with an irregular verb."

"Well, he acted very queer to me today." I told Benny all about it.

"Oh, my Lord!" Benny howled. "He probably wanted to interview you. I bet he mistook you for the famous one-legged French prostitute. She always uses white crutches."

"A pros—" but I couldn't even say the word. "One of those?" The very idea appalled me.

This was precisely the case.

I didn't regard the confusion as flattering. My idea of a prostitute was none too glamorous. I pictured a figure by Rubens, with a hip-swish like Sadie Thompson, packaged in sleazy satin and draped with a feather boa, and over it all a suffocating aroma of cheap perfume. Since then I have heard about and read the sketchy accounts of this same French prostitute's courageous activity and leadership in the Paris underground during the Nazi occupation, and I am quite proud of that brief mistaken identity.

CHAPTER XII

Wolves and Lambs

When I returned from Europe, the ship had scarcely scraped its dock before I began worrying because I didn't have a job. Actually, a solvent family, a comforting number of generous friends, and a reasonable chance of earning my own living, stood firmly between me and starvation. But I had the quaint notion that if I didn't get on a pay roll promptly, my only alternative was the bread line, with a vitamin deficiency, scurvy, and the immediate decalcification of all my bones.

Carefully preserved throughout my journey was a letter in my purse which introduced me, with some flattering phrases, to the field secretary of a large national girls' organization whose headquarters were in Chicago. I had operated for four summers on the Pacific Coast as a counselor in the camps of this organization. According to the Los Angeles executive, my work was highly satisfactory. She had used me in various capacities—camp craft, handcraft, swimming, hiking, etc. The children liked me and I had no discipline problems. Aside from the fact that I couldn't light a fire by rubbing two sticks together and wasn't particularly quick-tongued at naming all the feathered friends who winged over, I had an honorable record behind me.

In fact, the Los Angeles executive was sufficiently impressed to express the opinion that I had something of a talent for leading the young. She encouraged me to consider seriously the possibility of a career in her organization. With this in mind, she equipped me with the introduction and suggested that I stop over in Chicago on my return long enough to discuss the matter with the national executive.

Although I had gotten an alluring sniff of printer's ink and fancied the idea of flourishing a press card in the faces of policemen guarding recently murdered corpses, I still was not averse to considering an offer along more uplifting lines. The national economy, as well as my own, being what it was, I was eager, in fact, to consider anything. I squandered two days in Chicago for this mission.

With due respect for my first interview, I scrubbed myself into a fine scent and shine, manicured my nails, gargled Listerine, touched my face chastely with makeup, arrayed myself in tailored navy blue with the traditional touches of starched white, and went forth with my letter clutched in a properly gloved hand. I was not overconfident. In fact, I was terrified. But my qualms were only those of facing a new experience. I didn't actually expect to be hired on the spot, since jobs at that time were about as plentiful as crown jewels floating in the gutter. But I thought the chances were fair that I would be turned down with sincere regret. I had seen a good many of the sturdily built spinsters in their healthy shoes and middy blouses who gave forth their light in the name of this organization. Frankly, I felt that the sight of me, sleek and slim and all abloom with red corpuscles, might even inspire the lofty national secretary into a few ladylike cheers.

I was completely unprepared for the blasting brush-off I got. I've never experienced one like it since, I am glad to say. I hope no other handicapped person in the world ever emerged from his first job interview as thoroughly banged up emotionally as I was. Three or four such shiny moments in a row would have settled me permanently in a back room cutting out paper dolls. The incredible aspect of the situation was not that the Leader of Youth sincerely believed that it would be impossible for me to carry one of her torches on crutches, but that she told me off with a hiss that would have done credit to a desert diamond-back rattlesnake.

I handed her my letter in the reception room where she was introduced to me by one of her henchmen. She had just returned from luncheon—an interlude which I suspect she spent stuffing herself with chocolate éclairs. It may even have been indigestion, not malice, that motivated her.

She did not invite me into her office, nor did she sit down or suggest that I sit down. I was all primed modestly to mention my I.Q., my college honors, my church affiliation, and the names of several sterling characters who thought I was just dandy. But she didn't ask me any questions. She scanned the letter briefly and dropped it on a table. Then she let me have it with two guns, shot straight from her generous hips.

She told me that with my horrible handicap I should never for a moment consider an active job that involved leadership of young people or contact with the public. Her implication was not only that I was halt, but that the very sight of me would warp a sensitive young mind.

In frantic haste to justify my mad entertainment of such ridiculous heresy, I tried to tell her how fast I could swim, how far I could hike, and all about my four summers in camp and the serenely happy and uncomplicated reactions of all the children I had shepherded.

I didn't talk very well because there was a sob suffocating its lonely self in my tight throat. I finally left and walked twenty-two blocks to my hotel rather than get in a taxi and let the driver see me cry.

Feverishly I condemned my father, Mr. Fultz, my high school teachers, and my college professors for misleading me with the ludicrous myth that I had not only a fair, but a better-than-average chance for success in the economic world.

This woman who had so brashly told me the Truth was the head of an organization founded on Christian principles whose sole purpose for existence—aside from supplying salaries to her and others of her ilk—was helping girls who were not many years younger than I. Where else could I possibly expect a gentler reception and a more cautiously kind letdown than right there?

The very thought of what a hard-boiled newspaper editor would say to me when I brazenly asked him for a job terrorized my nights. If I had only started out on one of those hard-boiled editors, what a difference it would have made in my psychology! I've been turned down by some of the reputably toughest and most artistically blasphemous editors in the business, but not one of them ever took the spring out of my step and sent me home to sop up my tears in a pillow. Compared to that first female werewolf who bared her teeth at me, the editors were a frolicking bunch of cozy, cuddly lambs.

When I finally got home to Los Angeles, I was scared of my one-legged shadow. I bit my tongue with my chattering teeth many a time during the next month while I job-hunted. Nobody advertised for help in those days. Father gave me exclusive use of his car and I drove all over Southern California, apologetically peddling my talents to suburban and small-town newspapers.

I am sure I don't know how many—if any—editors turned me down because I used crutches. None of them inflamed my nerves by admitting to that point of view anyway. They all put whipped cream and maraschino cherries on their refusals. Everyone gave me a real hearing, comfortably seated, with plenty of time and advice thrown in free.

One editor did hint that the crutches might prove a hindrance to my career, but he made the comment under the most comforting circumstances possible. "One of my reporters is leaving to be married in three months," he told me. "I'll hold the job for you, unless you let me know that you're satisfactorily located elsewhere by that time."

Then he went on: "I think you'd do very well here. This is a small town and I imagine you make friends readily. I'd like to have you work for me. You'd never get anywhere on this paper, however. There's just no place to get, and I expect you have large ambitions. Frankly, I think you should be advised that a big metropolitan daily probably would hold your crutches against you in a straight reportorial job. It's a pretty lively business."

He could have told me I was cross-eyed at that point, however, and it wouldn't have ruffled me a bit. He was my dream man—dear old septuagenarian that he was, with his bald pate and silver-rimmed spectacles. He'd offered me a job with a salary. Twenty dollars a week—for that he could burn me on an altar, if he had a mind to.

I didn't have to wait for that job, however. Three days later the California Newspaper Publishers Association notified me that the *Citizen* in Covina, twenty miles from Los Angeles, needed a reporter. I phoned for an appointment with the editor James Wickizer, a young man fresh from the Columbia School of Journalism and determinedly precise and full of progressive ideas. He practically swore me in on a style book.

Two hours later I sat down at a typewriter and began knocking out the most dangerous of all small-town copy, the society news (pink—pink—pink—flowers, candles and ice cream). I rented a spare bedroom for fifteen dollars a month from the local sheriff's wife, opened a bank account with the fifty dollars Father gave me for a stake in life, and, poor fool that I am, I've been self-supporting ever since.

I never did forge ahead to my ambition—a by-line on a front-page murder story in the *New York Times.* I was detoured by a variety of positions that were laid out on salvers and served to me. I stayed just a year on the newspaper and then went back to Claremont, my college town, to marry my professor and take a proffered job in the Admissions Department of Scripps College. There, subsequently, I also assisted Dr. Mary Eyre, a psychologist, with a mental hygiene clinic and a child-guidance center.

I doubt if the editors of large metropolitan dailies tossed sleeplessly when I was lost to the newspaper world. They probably never would have flung themselves at my foot with pleas that I work for them. But I did discover during my year of reporting that the handicap was a help, not a hindrance, to my trade.

In the first place, crutches are very disarming. They seem to have unique power to open close mouths. Women bared their secrets to me and cheerfully ripped the garments off their neighbors' souls as well. Nobody likes to turn a crippled person away from a door—not without first inviting him in to rest a bit. They asked me questions until we were cozy. Then I asked them questions and they invariably opened up.

On a few occasions I went into Los Angeles, to cover stories with a local tie-in, where I ran into the resistance and competition that characterizes city reporting. I could slip in without struggle where a pair of muscular legs wouldn't have carried a kicking prize fighter.

I once stood at a carefully guarded door with the exasperated and frustrated press. The granite Horatio with the police badge didn't look as if a tender emotion could possibly sprout on his hard surface, but he reached out with his nightstick and touched me on the shoulder.

"There's a chair right inside here if you'd like to sit down while you wait."

I didn't want to sit down—or wait. What I did want terribly was a sprinter's chance at the corridor on the other side of the entry. I hesitated, however. It certainly was a situation offering unfair advantage. Honor reared its haloed head.

A tweedy-looking mess standing next to me gave me a poke. "I suppose you're not tired, you sucker!" he whispered out of the corner of his mouth that wasn't occupied by pipe or chewing gum. He was a remarkable person—he could chew and smoke simultaneously. "You're young, kid, but you're never going to make a newspaper woman if you don't get in that door, rest your fanny for five seconds on that chair, and then take off. That lump isn't going to chase you because in the first place his feet hurt and in the second place he knows we'll all storm in if he does. He won't shoot you, dearie—you're a doe."

"Oh, my—" I whispered back. "But what will everyone think?"

"They're probably planning to use crutches next time themselves."

"Thanks very much—I would like to sit down," I

said and walked through the entrance. My friend Baggy Tweeds was right. I touched my *derrière* to the chair to make it legal.

"I'm rested now," I announced forthrightly, just to give the sergeant a fighting chance, and then I was off and quite unpursued.

The reporters approved, apparently. They all yelled, "That's a girl!"

"She's only on a stinking little country sheet anyway," someone said. "That guy in the D.A.'s office is from her town. They probably don't go to press till next Thursday."

That was right on the nose. The L.A. papers had the story on the street three days before our paper was laid out in the forms. But nobody can ever argue me out of the conviction that crutches aren't a handy accessory to a reporter's costume.

And now, page Ripley! That blasting initial interview I had in Chicago netted me a job. It was the damned-out crutches that did it, too. I had been performing on the newspaper for only a few weeks when I got a letter, postmarked New York, from a total stranger. A minor and more benign executive who had overheard that fatal brush-off repeated it, in substance, to an acquaintance. She picked precisely the proper ears into which to pour her story. A two-crutch man himself, Edward Hungerford of the New

York Central Railroad, regarded me, I suspect, as a cause. Any insult to crutch-users stirred his fighting blood like a battle hymn.

He wrote me, sight-unseen, that he was building an organization to stage "Wings of a Century," a big transportation pageant at the Century of Progress and that he felt there might be a place for me if I were interested. He would interview me on his next trip to California and in the meantime, if I cared to consider his offer, please submit credentials. I submitted.

Two years later when the big bulldozers moved in on Michigan's lake front, I moved in on Chicago. It was a swell job. I worked on publicity and watched the Fair sprout out of the barren ground, and flower.

Among a few things that I learned from the Century of Progress, I will pass one profitable trifle on to posterity. A one-legger can make a fool out of a weight guesser. Scattered around the midway and in odd corners of the fairgrounds were a smattering of minor concessionaires whose equipment consisted of a swing-like seat attached to a set of scales, a stack of two-pound boxes of stale candy, and some horrible pallid Kewpie dolls, plus the brains in their heads. These bright boys offered, for a price, to guess your weight within three pounds. Failing to do this, they paid off in their pretty premiums. Their technique was to feel the arms of their victims, look pensive a minute, and then state the approximate avoirdupois. They didn't throw their weights around either. They were hitting very close to the bull's-eye.

There is nothing so hard as a crutch user's biceps. He walks on his arms, and it's fine exercise for developing muscle. I've often wished wistfully that I had an excuse to pack a wallop to someone's jaw, just to test my own strength.

The first weight guesser who fell into my trap was collecting quarters at a great rate and hanging onto his horrible wares. I stepped up and he felt my arm and gave me a respectful bow. "Solid," he announced.

He made no allowances for my soft places—and he apparently didn't consider just how much a well-set-up gam weighs. He guessed me 132 pounds—just 27 pounds over.

I played every weight guesser on the grounds, for a sucker. The winnings, however, a carload of ghastly chalky grinning Kewpies and the inedible chocolates, were hardly worth the effort.

It was at the Fair in Chicago that I met an engineer who built for me what he called "The Royal Nonesuch ne Plus Ultra Pedal Coordinator" for my car. This kindly genius decided that although I drove a standard car skillfully, using the technique of throwing my car out of gear, before pushing on the foot brake, that both the public and I would be considerably safer if my clutch and brake were coordinated. This was prior to the marketing of the Bendix free-wheeling device which, in spite of some weaknesses, subsequently proved a boon to one-legged drivers.

With a great deal of trouble and expense, and with clever ingenuity, my friend invented, built, and installed a brake and clutch coordinator in my car. It was designed to fit a Model A Ford and was highly successful, but unfortunately it was not transferable to another make. I did, however, have Bendix install free-wheeling in a Chevrolet that I owned later.

At the present time I drive a car with standard equipment. Come the millennium, however, I hope to possess the new Oldsmobile with the best of all devices for safe one-legged operation—the hydramatic drive. The Cadillac, to which I frankly don't aspire, also has this exceedingly efficient feature.

Insurance companies are a bit cool in their reception of handicapped drivers. Even with a spotless record and a fistful of operators' licenses from a variety of states staring them in the face, they are reluctant to write policies for one-legged drivers. I have always managed to get coverage, but I have shopped around for it and I have gone through some devilishly contrived tests to prove my skill.

The handicapped drivers that I know, all share my exceptional caution behind the wheel of a car. They realize, as I do, that in a court case, a one-legger would have a tough time convincing a jury that he wasn't at fault, irrespective of the circumstances of accident. The new automatic clutch in the Oldsmobile and the Cadillac should eliminate this prejudice completely.

CHAPTER XIII

Reading and Writing and Pig Latin

THERE was one profession to which I never gave serious thought during that preemployment period when I digested the Want Ads along with my breakfast coffee. That was school teaching. In fact, to insure myself permanently against such a fate, I had carefully avoided in college all courses labeled "Education." The one symbol of achievement that I didn't aim to hang in my study, alongside my deer antlers, was a teacher's certificate. Also, after the advice handed me so vehemently during my first job interview, I regarded it as providential that I had never aspired to a career of wielding the ruler.

But I stumbled into teaching when my husband was asked to take over the headmaster's position at Norton, a boarding and day school for small boys, in the country just outside Claremont, California. I am not sure just how capable I was as a teacher. I've never had a chance to make a survey of the adult spelling and punctuation of my charges, but I do know, in spite of that harsh warning I had, I didn't leave the landscape littered with little twisted minds.

The only twisting that was done was by the boys. They twisted me around their little fingers. I'm always a fool for a handsome man, and I discovered I was a complete pushover for the particular brand of charm peddled by males between the ages of eight and fourteen. Even with a toad in grubby hand and a snake crawling out of a corduroy pocket, any little disheveled ten-year-old could sell me an ice concession in Greenland.

I am convinced that the most delightful method of being driven crazy is by a horde of small boys. Their consistent clatter and vocalizing proved even more musical to my ears than my formerly top-tune favorite —the roar of presses.

It wasn't the teaching itself that I liked so much—it put an awful tax on my spelling—or the salary, which was negligible. It was just that I met so many interesting people and it was all so broadening and educational. I learned to associate in a manner quite cozy with snakes, and in pure self-defense, I developed a fancy for crawling things and white mice. I was taught to spin a top and shoot a fair game of marbles. I learned to speak fluent Pig Latin and Op, a much more erudite language. I also learned that a face like a Botticelli angel was a thing of beauty but not necessarily a joy forever. A head that would have looked perfectly natural with a halo cocked over it, could, I discovered, contrive most delightful and devilish mischief.

This idyllic job had the slight disadvantage of requiring duty approximately twenty-five hours a day, and it also necessitated, for purposes of noble example, consumption of vast quantities of oatmeal and other healthy, uninteresting delicacies. But the life was too active to encourage fat, and I was too entranced to be wearied by my long hours.

Such was my enthusiasm for this kind of punishment that I insisted upon being flailed in the summertime too. I pooled my strength with that of two masters and ran a camp for boys at Lake Arrowhead—Camp Robin Hood—complete with lethal weapons, bows and arrows.

I have a friend, only very slightly handicapped by infantile paralysis, who is a magnificent teacher. She didn't choose teaching as a profession because, like so many girls, nothing more imaginative occurred to her. She decided to teach because it was the one thing she wanted most to do. That rare attitude of mind, I am convinced, should have influenced every school board in the country to barter for her services. She is now a successful instructor in a large metropolitan system where she has thoroughly proved her merit. But she had a long and discouraging struggle getting a job—for no reason except a slight weakness in her knees. A childhood illness resulted in disability and disfigurement that was so slight as to be negligible. A twenty-four-legged muscular centipede, miraculously endowed with the mind of a genius, couldn't give more lavish gifts to children. But for a number of years, it looked as if she'd never have a chance to distribute her gifts. There is a tendency to scream for normalcy in the public school systems. Handicapped teachers are more likely to be found in the more resilient private school organizations.

I am, of course, not in a position to argue against this prejudice by presenting statistically reliable evidence. All I can say is that the young boys I taught took my handicap in their stride. They gave it little if any thought. Similarly they took in their stride the handicap of another member of our teaching staff.

The most thoroughly beloved and most successful master we had, was a young and vigorous man who had one crippled foot, victimized by polio. The boys admired, with the typical enthusiasm of their age group, the strong-legged athletic young men who supervised their play hours, but they loved the master who carried the physical handicap and who also carried a much more damaging handicap to popularity—the school master's weightiest burden, the teaching of Latin.

It was not perverted sympathy either, that prompted

their devotion. The master was completely worthy in every respect to be top favorite with his students. The lameness had no bearing one way or another on his position in the hearts of the boys. His attractiveness of personality, his rich understanding, and his skill and discipline in the classroom, would have made him a fine teacher, without his handicap; they made him an equally fine teacher with his handicap. In fact, his disability may even have enhanced his value as a teacher in a subtle way that perhaps was neither recognized by himself nor his pupils. I feel sure that the children in their natural experience of identifying themselves with this thoroughly beloved teacher achieved an understanding attitude toward the handicapped person in general that no amount of instruction or moralizing would have implanted.

Also, should it happen that any of these boys in later life suffered some disability themselves, there is no doubt that their mental recovery and acceptance would be more rapid and complete because of the fortification of the memory of this well-adjusted, happy, useful man.

To me, the following incident significantly demonstrates a schoolboy's attitude toward a handicapped teacher. Recently I happened to run onto one of our old Norton students, now grown into quite impressive manhood. Our conversation inevitably led to this favorite master.

"I hear he's married now," the boy said, "and has a bunch of kids. I bet he's a swell father. I've never had a teacher who held a candle to him."

"He was remarkably active for a man with a handicap, too," I added, with the cold-blooded intention of prodding for an opinion on this subject.

"Why, that's right—" The boy looked quizzical. "He *was* lame, wasn't he?"

I certainly do not follow this idea through with the recommendation that all handicapped people promptly start plugging for school-teaching jobs. I merely subscribe to the theory that, granted the qualifications of personality and training which make a normal person a good teacher, a physically handicapped person is at no disadvantage. This point of view may be applied to any other profession as well.

Paradoxically, if a handicapped person is not basically warmhearted and likeable, his physical abnormality may prove an insurmountable mountain to him in the field of teaching. Children are likely to choose an obvious peg on which to hang their scorn. I once knew a teacher in my own early school years, who behind her back was referred to as "Old Droopy Eye." Even I, as a one-legged little girl who should have had more natural compassion for a handicapped person, called her that without any consciousness of irony.

She had an injured muscle in her right eyelid that

gave her a permanent semi-wink, but her personality was such that she never for a moment misled anyone into thinking her merely flirtatious. She was a veritable tartar, with not a modicum of softness in her nature. She shouldn't have been a teacher. She probably knew her grammar book by heart, and I don't doubt she could spell every word in *Webster's Unabridged,* but she didn't like children. I think it would have given her the greatest pleasure to hang her entire class by their thumbs. We pupils felt this and returned the sentiment with enthusiasm. Since we subconsciously wanted to identify the source of our hatred, we hooked it on her defect and called her "Old Droopy Eye."

A psychologist friend of mine tells me that this is a fairly common tendency in children and is called "mechanism projection." If the hate had not been present anyway for some more valid reason, the defect would not have awakened it.

Of course, my schoolboys took a certain amount of interest in my crutches—an interest identical with that displayed in my childhood by my contemporary playmates. It was the inevitable young enthusiasm for anything that remotely resembled a vehicle on which to ride. The taller boys walked with my crutches and the smaller boys stood on chairs, leaned their weight in the saddles and swung off into space—quite an exciting sport. All sizes and varieties of boys tried to imitate my use of the crutches—as stilts.

They were not beyond playing tricks on me either—a sort of harmless clipping of my wings. It was regarded as something of a clever maneuver to kidnap my crutches without my knowing it. This was no small accomplishment since I am inclined to have them at my side constantly, and my mind if not my hand usually rests on them most of the time. The boys played this little game merely out of mischief—not meanness, as proved by the fact that they always posted a benevolent guard on me to be sure that I didn't need the crutches during the abduction. I contend that the very fact that they invented this nonsense at all was a healthy sign. They didn't hold my crutches in any awe or undue reverence. If they had, they would have ignored them completely with the most contrived and thoroughly false disinterest.

The boys took some pride in my accomplishments, demanding that I demonstrate my one-legged physical feats to new boarders. In this spirit, one of the more memorable athletic contests staged at Norton was a crutch race that had all the fanfare of an Olympic competition.

We had a physical education coach who ran the 440 and the 880 for the Los Angeles Athletic Club. He banged up an ankle and was temporarily outfitted with a pair of my crutches, on which he was exceptionally adept for a temporary time-server. It occurred to one of the boys that under the circumstances, a race between this damaged Mercury and me would be a fair and amenable contest—his skill as a trackman pitted against my skill on crutches.

The bounds were laid out—a one-hundred-yard dash. With a good deal of solemn officialism, the boys set us off with a blank pistol shot. Our four crutches and two feet pranced down the course. It wasn't really a fair contest. A lifetime of two-footed running isn't good preparation for a one-legged sprint. I won, but just by the front freckle on my nose. I don't think I ever felt more of a genuine heroine, however. I know how a laurel wreath must feel on a noble brow.

"Jeepers!" one small spectator remarked with awe. "She beat him, and he's a state champ." The little boy had apparently put out of his mind completely the rather unusual aspects of my victory.

CHAPTER XIV

So Much in Common

THERE is a certain freemasonry among amputees. I am always interested in meeting others of my species. Whether or not I coveted such encounters, however, I could hardly escape them. Friends, absolutely puffy and plumy over their cleverness, are constantly digging up one-legged people for me. With all the pride of a prospector bragging about knocking his pick against a vein of solid gold, they reveal their discovery.

"Oh, my dear, you know the other day I met a girl who only has one leg." They usually begin in some such manner. "I don't know her really, of course, but I asked her to come to tea so that you two can meet. You're certain to be great friends. You have so much in common."

In some respects this is just as adept socially as tossing off a party to which only persons who have had their appendices removed are invited. It's true the appendix-bereft would have quite a bit to say to each other. "My Doctor says . . ." ". . . never saw a worse case in my life." "Under anesthetic two hours . . ." ". . . what I suffered." "You should see my scar! . . ."

Appendicitis may be an excellent ice-breaker but it's only worth a one-night stand as a feature attraction. It's not a sound basis on which to build a beautiful friendship. The same is true of amputations. Accident like appendicitis is no respector of personalities. There is no assurance at all that just any two amputees who collide at a cocktail party will promptly become boon buddies, after their exchange of surgical detail. I don't recommend such a criterion for picking intimates. It's better to plod along in the old-fashioned way, depending upon personal rapport and common interests to determine permanent friendships, and take the handicaps where they happen to fall.

However, I still recommend welcoming every opportunity to meet others with similar handicaps. Sometimes cordial enduring amity does develop from these encounters. And although occasionally just the opposite is true—you run smack into torpor—it's still worth the chance. Invariably the preliminaries, at least, are entertaining: the swapping of life stories, the inevitable arguments: artificial-leg users *vs.* crutch addicts, the discussions of walking gear and techniques. Very often casually encountered members of the clan have made great contribution to my comfort by their suggestions—and I hope, vice versa.

SO MUCH IN COMMON

I met the first of "my own kind"—another one-legged girl—when I was about twelve. A week before this meeting, a rancher friend of Father's drove in from the country and called at our house. He told us that some of his Kansas kin were coming out to California on a visit. "The little girl's about your age," he explained to me, "and she's 'that way,' too." Mother looked slightly pained. "You two kiddies ought to hit it off just fine," he said.

A date was set for me to spend a whole day at the ranch. This would have been thrilling enough in itself, but combined with the anticipation of meeting a one-legged "kiddy" from Kansas, my excitement simply couldn't be cooped.

Forthrightly, I even warned my best friend, Barbara Bradley, that the chances were she couldn't be my best friend much longer. Her days of such honor were numbered, as she could well understand herself. This single-cylinder Kansan and I were just bound to become bosom chums immediately.

The day I went to the country, my hair was tightly braided in pigtails and then pinned around my head, and my face was scrubbed to a shine. I wore blue denim overalls, all fresh and clean, and a blue shirt. This was my favorite costume, and it had been purchased for just such occasions. Ranch life was always rough on my clothes since I liked to slide on hay, ride astride the sweaty backs of plow horses, cuddle up to piglets and other barnyard young, and generally make a dirty mess of myself.

When I arrived I met the little Kansan. She turned out to be two years older than I was. She was fourteen, but even if we'd both been two-legged and were the same age, we'd have been a world apart in interests. As it was we had nothing in common but a couple of feet in Heaven, and they probably were dancing on gold pavements at opposite ends of the town.

She had lived on a middle-western farm most of her life, but it was I who resembled the farmerette. She was dressed in dainty sprigged muslin with a white slipper and stocking, and her hair was curled. I felt completely gauche in her presence.

She was very nice to me, however. She inquired politely about my accident and told me about hers. She had dashed out in the street, with no thought of life or limb, in pursuit of an endangered kitten and had been run down by an automobile. This made her extremely heroic and put me at a disadvantage. All I'd done, after all, was disobey my mother by borrowing an ill-fated bicycle. Also, every year or so she had to go back to the hospital in Kansas City and have an operation. The bone in her stump continued to grow and required periodic pruning. For some reason that I do not understand but for which I am grateful to an able small-town surgeon, I have never had this recurrent trouble, common to many children whose amputations occurred early in life. This periodic drama in the Kansan's life also made me feel inferior by contrast. "I had two stitches in my head," I bragged in my own defense, "when I fell out of a tree." I knew it wasn't much.

More tedious, she wanted me to sit in a chair while she performed at the piano. She executed (by slow torture) a number called "Memories." Since my sister played the same ditty day and night at home, this wasn't exactly exciting to me who laid no claim to the appreciation of either music or romance. We finally went outside where we sat sedately under a tree and ate grapes. I amused myself by seeing how many I could stuff in my mouth at once, and the pretty little Kansan amused herself by watching the road—for the neighbor boys, I suspect.

I spent a miserable day, and when I got home was greeted by Mother with the startled words, "My goodness, you're clean! Didn't you have a good time?"

I called up Barbara Bradley right away and assured her she was still my stanchest comrade. "Why, that girl is just like my sister Bernice," I said. "I couldn't have anyone like that for my best friend."

It was a profound discovery I made that day—that one-leggedness may occur anywhere. It was like blue eyes or brown hair. It had nothing to do with congeniality. The idea startled me, since I somehow had labored under the illusion that all one-legged girls would be exactly like me; braces on the teeth, freckles on the nose and all.

I have met a great many crippled people since then and some of them have developed into real friends. Even the most casual contacts, however, have been rewarding. One-leggedness is a common ground on which individuals of vast difference in background can meet and communicate. I have had fascinating conversations with handicapped persons whose lives were so divergent from my own that in the normal course of a two-legged life, I never even would have crossed their pathways.

A jolly drunk who sold newspapers on a city corner and who happened to wear a peg leg, gave me a full, though perhaps slightly alcohol-flavored, account of himself one day while I waited for a bus. Similarly, I've learned all about the private lives of a taxi driver, an ex-policeman, a sculptor, a factory worker out on parole from a woman's reformatory, a little one-armed Negro orphan, a Japanese fruit peddler, an architect, etc., etc. We speak to each other. We flaunt our fraternity badges. Whatever our limping walks in life we are all people of parts—missing. We stand on common ground. We may remain transients; we usually do. We meet; we pass on; but we enrich each other in the passing.

There are two classes of amputees that I make

particular effort to meet. Others I merely take as they come. I always try to acquaint myself with newcomers to the freemasonry, and recently maimed. Then I am probably as obnoxious as a first grader who has learned to spell "cat" and lords it over his little brother who is still in kindergarten. I pass out advice with the assurance of an established seer. However, I know from experience the value of a veteran's suggestions to the recruit. I regard my knowledge as inherited wealth that I am obliged to preserve, increase, and pass on to the next generation. Often I correspond with the recently handicapped in an effort to give encouragement during the inevitable anguish that precedes adjustment to the new way of life.

In addition to the recently handicapped, from the grossest commercial motive, I am always on the prowl for females of the species who have missing left legs and who wear a size 5½ B shoe. Here is a solid foundation on which to construct sodality. We exchange our odd shoes.

Ruth Rubin, an enterprising woman in St. Louis, a trained nurse, has as her imaginative and helpful hobby, a shoe exchange. She encourages one-leggers to write in their shoe sizes and mates up feet all over the country. My foster foot, for instance, lives in Burbank, California. The enterprise operates on the principle of a shoe for a shoe.

This exchange proved especially useful to me during

shoe rationing. Unipeds are inclined to be more destructive to footwear than ordinary people, since their entire weight rests in one shoe. Moreover, to maintain their balance, amputees tend to grab the earth harder with their single foot. With the limited number of shoe coupons provided, I would have been a scuffy-toed derelict if it hadn't been for the shoe exchange which kept me in slick footwear for the duration. My contributions similarly kept someone else well shod. The pleasant economy of such a scheme is obvious.

There are other organizations that cater to the disabled. Most of these are founded on the premise that the handicapped need each other. They do—especially during their period of adjustment. Many of these fraternities publish little magazines that circulate among the handicapped and publicize the stories of the members. Such publications are *Outwitting Handicaps*, the *Spot-Lite, Courage*, etc. They carry also an advertising section devoted to artificial legs and arms, stump socks, Ampu-Balm, wheel chairs, and other equipment for amputees. Most of these organizations exact a small membership fee or contribution which pays for the magazine and frequently for a variety of other helpful services: employment advice, advice on prosthesis, providing correspondence companions for hospitalized patients, etc.

A few of the organizations are completely free, the

service being the friendly contribution of some humanitarian hobbyist. For instance, a Hollywood man, Mr. Stuart Noble, although not handicapped himself, entertains great compassion and understanding for the disabled. For many years he has been interested in assisting amputees. He organized a club called The Good Friends, and he has devoted a great deal of time and money to assisting the handicapped in making happy adjustments to life—helping them find friends and employment, etc.

Edward Hungerford of New York, handicapped himself, collects crutch users who strike his fancy all over the country, and in a less formal way does the same thing for his collection that Mr. Noble does.

The most adequate and able of all the organizations, of course, is the National Society for Crippled Children and Adults, Inc. This society has forty-two well-organized official state affiliates, with some two thousand local chapters, and is based on the most intelligent and scientific approaches to the problems of the disabled. The magazine of this organization, *The Crippled Child,* features articles by recognized authorities on recovery methods, occupational therapy, rehabilitation, prosthesis, etc. This organization is financed by the annual national Easter-seal sales, by private subscription, and by state allotment of funds. A handicapped person in need of guidance of any sort would most wisely seek it here.

These organizations offer admirable encouragement and practical assistance to many disabled. In my opinion, their greatest service is to the newcomer to the clan, those who are groping "at the bottom of the worst" and who desperately need the fortification of others' experiences in recovery.

Once an amputee is well adjusted to life, there is of course no necessity for his seeking his associates among the similarly maimed. In fact, too prolonged an interest in a personal physical abnormality is likely to breed an unhealthy introversion or sentimentalism.

I have a uniped acquaintance who almost makes a profession of her handicap. I recognize this as a defense mechanism, but I don't condone it. She writes me long, six-page typewritten letters that are concerned from start to finish with her one-leggedness. She has been handicapped for many years. She is a contented wife, secure financially, equipped with a good mind, and in excellent health. I have gathered from her lengthy opera, however, that her one major interest in life is her physical abnormality. It's a strange perverted narcissism. If she would discuss some little feminine fripperies, flower arrangement, the breeding and care of canary birds, or methods for removing spots from fabrics—almost anything—I would continue writing to her. But I simply can't read six pages every two weeks devoted to her mental contortions over her long-buried extremity. It's like a widow conversationally digging up the remains of her twenty-year-deceased partner every time she gets you in a corner.

Not that my thoroughly one-legged friend is grim in her attitude. On the contrary, she makes a fetish of cheerfulness. Her handwriting practically beams at me. She has gained great spiritual strength from her suffering and she never forgets it or fails to remind me of her beautiful burning inner light. It embarrasses me acutely. You have spiritual strength or you don't have it—so what? It's as bad taste to mention it as it is to brag about ancestors or a bulky bank account. If it's there, spiritual strength, like good breeding, shows itself; also, like good breeding, it sickens and dies by the mere act of self-recognition and advertisement.

I know a young man who is blind and who graduated with honors from the same college from which I graduated without honors. He never mentioned his spiritual strength. He didn't mention his blindness either. He didn't have to, his blindness and his spiritual strength were equally obvious. This young man had been to a school for the blind. He associated with blind people long enough to adjust himself to the hardships of his life, but he didn't spend his time sitting around with the blind and discussing blindness. He had many enthusiastic interests and his friends, who were legion—the halt, the blind, or just plain standard merchandise—were those who shared his enthusiasms.

My philosophizing letter-writer also reminds me periodically of my obligation to her. "We have to stick together, we handicapped," she says. "The rest of the world doesn't understand us." I'll string along with the world; it understands me O.K.

It understands quite a few other one-legged people too. For instance, Herbert Marshall, the movie star—I wouldn't mind being on cozy terms with him. I think it might be absolutely lovely, but my interest isn't humanitarian. It has nothing to do with the fact that he wears an artificial leg and might need me to stick to him, poor thing, because the world doesn't understand him. Major Seversky has the world by the tail, too—and young Charles Bolte, the head of the new American Veterans Committee, swings along with the world even though his right side-kicker is timber. One-legged Laurence Stallings, the playwright, has an amenable relationship with the world, too. And what of the lovely-voiced Connie Boswell? Does the world fail to understand her songs because of her lack of legs?

I have a very dear one-legged friend who is attractive and interesting, and during the first ten minutes of our acquaintance she told me the circumstances of her accident and I told her the circumstances of mine. We have been friends for twenty years but our congeniality is completely detached from our common handicap. We don't mention it for years on end.

In fact, the only time that we are at all conscious of our similar state is when we go out somewhere and face the public together. I must say that in the aggregate, a crew of crutch-users limping into a big hotel dining room or a theater together create a stir that I don't enjoy. This young woman and I were both dinner guests one evening of a man who also used crutches. We marched through a popular crowded Hollywood restaurant, to the accompaniment of a terrific buzz. We might as well have been the Barrymores having a family reunion, except that nobody wanted our autographs.

"One family, do you suppose?" I heard someone whisper. "All hurt in the same accident—and all lost a leg! Did you ever hear of such a thing in all your life!" "Maybe it's congenital—he passed it on to his two daughters . . ."

It's funny, sure—funny as a crutch, as the saying goes.

Whoops!—when I entertain my crutch-borne friends, proud as I am of them, I'd rather bend over a hot stove all day than take them to a restaurant. They feel the same way I do. We've all learned to tolerate the casual curiosity we create alone, but en masse the curiosity is not casual. It's suffocating!

CHAPTER XV

Ski-doodling

When the California judge severed the matrimonial tie that was binding, I decided to go to New York. I entrained from Los Angeles decked out in some new grass widow's weeds, but I didn't feel much like a gay divorcee. I'd worn a ring on my finger and a ring in my nose so long, freedom didn't feel comfortable. I decided to take a year of graduate work at Columbia University because it was a long way from California. Although I entertained the usual maniacal idolatry of my native state, the place was suddenly cluttered with sentimental landmarks upon which I was frequently moved to shower mournful tears. Since the rainfall situation out there was adequate without my reinforcements, I decided to take my tears elsewhere.

Before actually enrolling at Columbia, I went forth and looked over a few of the more impressive secretarial schools in New York, the kind that serve their students a cup of tea in the afternoon and guarantee all graduates pink, plush jobs.

I, however, was different. I could buy my good little black dress from Saks, pay my tuition, and have my tea, but they wouldn't guarantee me placement.

One of the personnel interviewers asked me if she could be frank. She said she thought it would be a fine thing if I enrolled in her school (I think she figured the finger exercises would be good for me) but she feared she couldn't place me as a secretary.

"I don't think you'd be quite active enough—shall we say?—for the life."

"Shall we say that you let me be frank for a while?" I didn't make that crack, of course. That's what I wished I'd said after I got home.

Instead, in meek surrender, I went back up to Morningside Heights and enrolled in the School of Business at Columbia, signing up for an accelerated course in shorthand and typing offered yearly to twenty-five career-crazy college graduates. I felt like a jaded old hag among all the bright and eager just down from Smith and Wellesley. The placement service at Columbia had a much more hopeful attitude toward me. The counselor even rashly assured me that I would be easier to place than most, since I had had some experience, and that I could demand a better starting salary. She even got me a part-time job after class hours wasting stationery in one of the university offices.

I had regarded learning shorthand and typing as

a dull chore to be endured for the sake of the economic tool that would thereby be fitted to my hand. It turned out, however, to be very interesting to me. This was probably due entirely to the instructress, Miss Zilla McDonald, who really put buck and wing into her teaching methods. She was a versatile person who taught shorthand and typing by day and then at night wrote very charming books for children.

It was while I was in New York that I discovered in a small way just what happens to people who are unwise enough to get their pictures in the newspapers. Mother always had a theory that if you led the good life, you never got your photograph in the paper, unless you happened to be elected President of the United States, got married, or died honorably.

Well, I led the good life all right, within fairly generous bounds anyway, but I got my picture in a New York paper and it wasn't because I happened to be elected President of the United States. On the final analysis there was really no reason at all for this phenomenon.

Being a Californian, I had had no convenient opportunity to learn to ski. That winter in New York, however, I just happened to fall into a crowd who chattered on and on about wax and bindings and slalom races and Christies and a lot of other things that I still don't understand. All this talk went into my blood like a hopped-up transfusion. I too began watching the temperature and scanning the boards in Grand Central to see if any ski trains were scheduled.

Finally, one day I took the fatal step that was to land me on my fanny many a future time. I went into Best's and bought myself a neat but not gaudy ski suit, complete with a heavy cableknit turtle-neck sweater and a cap to match. It involved such a heavy expenditure that I couldn't afford not to use it. So, to protect my investment, I went to Macy's and bought skis, boots, trappings and a pair of ski poles. The latter were ripped to pieces by a skeptical but indulgent friend. He attached the ski-pole ends to a pair of my light-weight wooden crutches.

The first ski train that left New York that season had me on it with a crowd of my skiing friends and about five hundred other enthusiasts. We only went as far as Phoenicia. Off the train, one of my cohorts helped buckle on my lone ski, and I started pushing myself around with the crutch-ski poles to get the feel of it.

I wish I could say that before the winter was over I was coming down the memorial ski slide like a wind straight out of Scandinavia. Such was not the case, however. I finally got to the place where I could skim up and down the gentle slopes of a golf course, but that was all. Still, at least two fellow amputees have accomplished what I couldn't. Yves Gosselin, a student at Laval University at Lac Beauport, P. Q., and Bert Porter of Rutland, Vermont, both have proved that the downhill slalom can be executed with exceptional professional skill and speed by one-legged skiers. I had a lot of fun anyway, with my unimpressive ups and downs and got plenty of use out of the skiing togs—in fact, I practically wore the seat right out of the pants. However, on that first trip to Phoenicia, I wasn't even sure I could stand up on a ski. By the end of the day, I was sure on that point at least; I couldn't.

Since this was the opening day of skiing for New York, several of the newspapers sent photographers out to get human-interest shots of the winter frolickers. It seems that I was a human-interest shot.

Two photographers came up before I'd gotten a hundred yards from the train and asked if they could take my picture.

"For goodness' sake, why?" I asked.

"Because a girl with one foot who can ski is damned interesting," one of them said.

"Well, I can't ski," I said. "I've only had this ski on for five minutes and I haven't done anything impressive yet but fall down."

"Oh, that's O.K.," the photographer said. "You don't have to get technical about it."

"Go ahead and let him take your picture," my friends all urged.

"Why don't you wait until later?" I suggested. "Maybe I'll know how to ski in an hour or two."

"We can't wait till you learn to ski, we've got a deadline to meet."

Two photographers took my picture and so did a lot of unofficial stray sheep lugging Brownies. I could almost hear Father's voice booming clear across the continent. "Exhibitionist!"

Fortunately nobody I knew ever saw the picture. It wasn't in the *Times* or the *Herald Tribune.* But everyone I didn't know saw it.

The papers were already on the streets—or to be more precise, I should say in the subways—when we got back to New York. I got just the merest glimmer of what I was in for when we piled our skis into a cab to go home.

The cab driver turned around and said, "Je-*sus!* I was just wishing I could lay eyes on you, kid. I was just now looking at your picture in the paper. I sure would like to see you ski."

"Oh, that was all a terrible mistake," I apologized. "I can't ski."

"That's what you say. You're just modest. But the paper says different and that's good enough for me."

That was good enough for a lot of others as well.

When I got back to my apartment house the elevator boy was absolutely beside himself. I felt as if I'd gone out that morning an ugly duckling and returned a swan.

"Say, they got your picture in the paper! I was telling a guy, friend of mine, that I knew you real good and he didn't believe me. I said I sure knew you."

"Well, that's right, you sure know me real good," I agreed. "You can tell him I said so."

"Well, you see, this guy is skeptical. He says if I know you so good why don't I introduce him. He said two bucks I didn't know you at all. I said, 'Done.' "

"Where's your friend?" I sighed with resignation. "With that kind of money involved, you'd better bring him around."

"He's down to the poolroom on Amsterdam—just two blocks from here. I'm supposed to be off duty now, but I stayed on till you got back. But I'm not asking you to go down to a poolroom. I wouldn't ask that of you."

"I'm sure you wouldn't. We better go now, so that I can get back and see how many of my bones are broken."

He offered to split the two dollars with me, but I figured it wasn't really honest money, and I wouldn't touch a penny of it.

For the next two weeks everywhere I went elevator boys, butcher boys, Western Union boys, pouchy old boys, and just plain little boys nailed me. "Say, aren't you the lady that skis?"

I finally just answered "Yes." From then on I spent every week end I could at Great Barrington or Placid or any place that had enough snow for me to fall down in. I had to learn to ski. It was the only way to make an honest woman of me. It nearly killed me.

One of the most interesting encounters that resulted from that picture in the newspaper was my run-in with the law. I was walking along Fifth Avenue one afternoon when a big Irish policeman down the block took after me at a gallop. "Pardon me," he puffed when he caught up, "aren't you the lady that skis?"

"Well, sort of."

"I thought so." He grinned from ear to ear. "My sister has only one leg and she saw your picture in the paper and she said she'd sure like to meet you. She doesn't get around too well herself and she'd like to know how you possibly manage to ski. I told her I was sure I'd seen you on my beat once or twice right here on Fifth Avenue and that if I ever saw you again, I'd speak to you."

"I'd be very happy to meet your sister," I said. And then I remembered a conversation I'd had just that day with Jessie Fenton, a novelist friend of mine for whom I was doing some typing. She was threatening to go out and pick up a New York policeman because she needed some authentic background material for an arrest scene in her book *Down the Dark Street.* Here was the man for Jessie, complete with an amputee sister for me.

"Why don't you bring your sister and come up and call on me some evening?" I suggested, and I whipped out a card and wrote out my address. "Could you come on Tuesday?"

"Sure can!'

We had quite a party. Dr. and Mrs. Fenton came, and so did my current beau, who didn't approve of my picking up a policeman on Fifth Avenue.

"What's the matter with policemen?" I asked him. "You're just a glorified flatfoot with arch supporters yourself." He was with Army intelligence, a sort of a prewar cloak-and-dagger boy.

My roommate was also present to cast her gloomy disapproving countenance on the proceedings.

The sister was a charming young woman, and we spent most of the evening handing each other the usual sisterhood chitchat. Mrs. Fenton got all the answers for her arrest problem from thc policeman. He blushed with pride and began composing his sentences carefully when he realized that he was contributing to literature. He entertained us for the remainder of the evening with some lurid and amusing incidents from his twenty years' duty as one of New York's Finest. Even my roommate—even my beau—admitted that it was a most successful soirée.

A few days later the policeman delivered me a summons over the telephone. He said that he and his sister wanted to return my hospitality. I accepted promptly. They gave me dinner in a very nice restaurant off Washington Square. We had a pleasant time. The cop dropped his sister off at her apartment in the Village and drove me uptown alone.

It seemed that the policeman didn't want all one-legged girls to be sisters to him. He tried to put the long arm of the law around me. Thus ended a beautiful friendship.

CHAPTER XVI

"Having a Wonderful Time"

WHEN I went to New York, I had in mind for myself a flashy career right out of a woman's slick magazine plot. I would have an office on at least the fifty-ninth floor of a skyscraper and would get ahead so fast that vice-presidents would shiver over their breakfast coffee daily in fear that when they got to their offices I would have usurped their swivel chairs. Friends in California were going to hear about me clear across the continent and marvel and envy. "Just think—and we never really appreciated her genius. She lives in a penthouse now. . . ." I was going to be one of the noisiest trumpets in the Manhattan symphony, and wear a John-Frederics hat with a rose on top.

When I went in for my placement interview at Columbia, however, I was almost as startled as the counselor when I heard myself announce with burning sincerity that I'd like a job in the hinterland.

"Do you mean that you'd leave New York?" she demanded sternly, as if she were giving me a sobriety test.

"Yes," I said. "The subways smell. And I'd like to go some place where cultivation is on a larger scale than in the window boxes at Bonwit Teller. I'll live in the country and come back here on my vacations just to be quaint."

"Of course," the counselor warned me, "the opportunities for advancement probably won't be as plentiful if you take a job in a small town. I think you might be quite successful right here."

"You know," I said, "confidentially, I don't think I really want to get ahead. Yesterday I visited some bright young friends of mine. They've all got fascinating jobs and they are all forging ahead fast. They live five in one apartment. To get into their bathroom, you have to fight your way through damp stockings that are as thick as Spanish moss growing on old oaks in a Louisiana swamp. I'll take less money in a spot where it goes farther and where people sometimes stroll. Of course, I'd just as soon have a job that's interesting."

"Well, the Fels Research Institute at Antioch College in Ohio wants a secretary who can also edit their publications."

On my way to California for the summer, I stopped in Yellow Springs, Ohio, and had an interview with Dr. Sontag, the director of the Fels Research Institute. It is one of the leading child-study centers in the country, making a long-range inquiry into the effects of prenatal and postnatal environment. I wanted a job there very much.

Just to face the issue immediately and have it over with, I said to Dr. Sontag, "I hope that my handicap doesn't come as too great a shock to you. It really isn't hampering to me at all, and I assure you that you won't have to make any allowances for me in assignment of duties, if you should decide to give me a chance here."

Dr. Sontag, with dignified solemnity said, "As a physician there is very little that shocks me."

Had I known him better at the time, I would have recognized a slight shift in the level of his right eyebrow that implied amusement. If he had possessed a beard I am sure he would have chortled into it.

He hired me a few days later by telegram. When I returned to Ohio to take up my duties, I had a chance to see my reference letters that had been in the Doctor's possession when he interviewed me. There was no doubt; my handicap certainly didn't come as a surprise to him!

Every single reference letter went into flowery rhetoric about my physical condition. Curiously enough, the letters all treated my handicap like some kind of subtle virtue. It was dwelt upon much more fully than any of my good, sterling secretarial qualifications. The letters were flattering enough, but I still marvel that anyone ever hired me—as a secretary anyway—on the basis of them. They certainly weren't typical recommendations.

They contained choice eulogies similar to these: ". . . and she can carry a cup of hot tea across a room as gracefully as anyone else." ". . . she can chin herself sixteen times on a bar." (It didn't specify what kind of a bar.) ". . . this girl can actually beat me at tennis."

Ideally, the letters would have been most persuasive pleading the case of a somewhat bright slugger applying for a job as bouncer in a night club.

I asked Dr. Sontag whatever possessed him to take a chance on someone whose gentlest talent was carrying a cup of tea and who otherwise sounded thoroughly muscle bound and probably had two cauliflower ears concealed under her hat.

"I figured we could always use you to put down an insurrection." That was all the satisfaction I ever got out of him.

My job had everything I like best—except a big salary. However, money stretched twice as far in a village as it would have in New York. I could wear comfortable shoes to work and I didn't have to put on a hat in the morning and race for the subway, and nobody cared whether or not I had a good little black dress from Saks.

The staff at the research foundation and at the college were friendly and interesting people. The subjects of the study—about one hundred children of all sizes and shapes and varieties—breezed in and out of the offices on schedule to liven up my routine. The work was varied, and I learned all manner of fascinating things while I corrected the spelling and punctuation of the scientists who did the research and wrote the publications. When I looked out my office window, I saw green grass with crocuses pushing through it in the spring and red leaves lying on it in the fall. There was air enough for everyone to breathe deeply. The vacations were long, with pay. And the Antioch atmosphere was so thoroughly congenial and stimulating that many people exposed to it go through the remainder of their lives with a retrogressive psychosis—a wistful tendency forever to look back on "the good old days."

I am quite sure I would have grown old and toothless, but not rich, quite contentedly on that job, if I hadn't happened onto the one thing that had more appeal.

During my second summer's vacation, my college roommate, Lucile Hutton, came East and together we drove my car all over Quebec and Ontario in Canada and through New England. It was on Cape Cod, in Provincetown, that the feeling came over me strongly that maybe my job in Ohio didn't have absolutely everything. We stayed in Provincetown much longer than we had planned, while I humored this whim which wasted no time developing into a lifetime conviction.

I met a Man. I have met quite a few in my day, but this was different. It was a pick-up. Who picked up whom is still a moot family question. Anyway, we met in the Provincetown Museum and wasted at least an hour acting interested in old Sandwich glass and whalebones. We haven't yet been formally introduced, but we've gotten by all right on an informal basis.

I recognized the encounter as important. That very night I wrote a postcard to an attractive friend of mine in New York. "Having a wonderful time. Met a magnificent man in a museum. Terribly glad you aren't here."

She replied by postcard. "Is magnificent man in museum a mummy? If so, glad I'm not there too."

"Magnificent man not a mummy, but would make a fine pappy. I think his name is Herman, but that's all there is against him."

His name wasn't Herman. It was Sherman—so, all faults thereby eliminated, he turned out to be perfect. To indicate my complete enthusiasm for him, I must admit that I accepted his proposal of marriage while still believing him to be Herman.

I wasn't nearly as impetuous as he was, however. He didn't even have an approximation of my given name when he proposed. And he made his declaration, of necessity, at the top of his lungs.

We were riding horseback along the Cape Cod dunes. He suggested that we get off our horses, but since I was so unimpressive on the remount and didn't have a crutch with me, of course, I refused. I show a regrettable simple-mindedness at times.

In addition to my own lack of cooperation, another deterrant to romance was my horse. He didn't feel as friendly disposed toward the other horse, as I did toward the other rider. In fact, my unobliging nag stayed at least two lengths ahead or two lengths behind his stablemate.

Still "Herman" was a man of action who was determined to overcome all odds. He wished he knew my first name since he felt the situation might be cozier under the circumstances. But nothing could defeat him when his inspiration came.

He yelled down the dunes after me. "Mrs. Harris! Mrs. Harris!" he called. "Will you marry me?"

"Oh, Herman," I yelled back, "I would simply love to marry you and you may call me Louise, now that we are formally engaged."

"And you may call me Sherman, if you want to," he said. "That's my name."

So I did, and he did—and three months later we were married.

The only reason we waited that long was because my father sent me a stern parental wire. "Insist you get acquainted with this stranger before marrying him."

As I said to Father, "You just don't know how easy it was to get acquainted with him. Besides, I'm terribly good at it."

CHAPTER XVII

In Praise of a Peg Leg

SHERMAN was born in Norfolk, Virginia, but since his father was a naval officer who merely happened to be stationed there at the time of this most blessed event, Sherman can't really claim the honest status of a fine old Southern Gentleman. The one thing he got from Virginia, he says, was a discriminating taste for mint juleps. This seems a bit precocious, since he left there at the age of six months, but I never question his talents. As a Navy junior, his life was a roving one. He did spend his preparatory school and college years in New Jersey, but he never legally adopted any locality until he got old enough to have an effective mind of his own. Then he chose himself a state and became much more tiresome about it than a native. He selected Arizona.

In his enthusiasm for the place, he showed a mild touch in the head, quite similar to the psychosis that frequently afflicts Californians and Texans with their typical spells of wild, frenzied exultation over their native soil. When I met Sherman, he was only in the

East vacationing with his family. I was not for a minute allowed to forget that he was still young Lochinvar out of the West.

When he did his courting, he polished off two jobs simultaneously. He wooed me effectively and at the same time sold me Arizona. In fact, frequently his double-threat technique was a little confusing. If he spoke highly and with passionate warmth of the color "blue," for instance, there was no point in my fluttering my lashes. He was likely to be transported over the Arizona sky, not my eyes. And curves, well, they might be mine, but more probably he was describing some road high in the Chiricahua Mountains, 2500 miles from me. It was a little disconcerting but now and again he'd toss good old Tray a nice bonus and I was content.

He snared me in both traps. I not only was anxious to marry him, I was dying to be a Pioneer Woman in Arizona. If I couldn't actually mold the course of empire, I at least could paint the walls and hang some gingham curtains in the adobe house that Sherman had out there, plunk in the middle of a terrific, overpowering piece of scenery.

He was very forthright with me, before he lured me away from my typewriter and into the wilderness.

"How do you feel about public utilities?" he asked.

"Well," I said, "if you are inquiring about my dowry,

I own two common stocks in Pacific Gas and Electric. The income keeps me in chewing gum."

"No, that wasn't what I had in mind," he said. "I just wondered if you had any special attachment for running water, piped gas, electricity, and telephones."

"Water, I like. I don't abstain. I'll take a drink with the best of them," I said, "and I do like my meat seared on the outside."

"We'd have water, of course. There's a fine well and lots of heat but it comes from a fireplace and a coal cookstove."

"For goodness' sake," I assured him lightheadedly, "that takes care of everything."

"Except plumbing," he added ominously.

But I wasn't one to let hot and cold running water and a flush toilet interrupt the course of true love.

Sherman drove West in a new car and I went out a few weeks later on the train. He met me in New Mexico and we were married.

We lived in an adobe house, a former ranger station in the Dragoon Mountains, long abandoned by the Forest Service. We paid five dollars a month for it. We had eighty acres of land, two horses who came galloping up when we rang a dinner bell, and a cow named Pearl (the variety that should be cast before swine). She was always kicking the bucket, but by that I don't mean she died. She wasn't that obliging. I still don't like milk.

We also had twelve hens named for flowers. We couldn't distinguish Arbutus from Marigold, however. They all looked alike, except one that turned out to be a rooster. But he died violently early in life. The only problem connected with this anonymity was that when we stewed one of the girls, we never knew which blossom we'd plucked.

We were forty-five miles from pavement, three miles from our postbox, twenty-six miles from the grocery store, and seven miles from a friendly neighbor. We did have a neighbor five miles away but he wasn't exactly cordial. He had the annoying habit of shooting at us.

Everything Sherman told me about Arizona was true. The place positively reeked of fresh air. It was hand in glove with Nature, and everything Nature did around the place she did in a big way. There were tremendous mountains propped up all over the horizon. When the sun shone, it seared. When the rains came, they flooded. When the winds blew, they sounded like Niagara Falls torrenting down our canyon. When the furry friends in the forest made noises, they screeched because they were wildcats and mountain lions. It was all quite violent, and when I got over a slight nervous breakdown caused by finding a rattlesnake on my front doorstep one day and discovering a mountain lion on my roof one night, I quite liked it. I'd have made a fine wife for Daniel Boone.

The coal stove and I didn't hit it off like soulmates from the start. We didn't read life's meaning in each other's eyes. I had to get onto her dietary habits and finally learned just the proper mixture of tinder for her tastes and how much coal to shovel into the ravenous, gaping black mouth. She was allergic to wood and smoked like a dragon when it was forced upon her as a quick snack.

I finally became the master—or, at least, I thought I was the master. The stove, however, was a villain at stomach (she had no heart). She had a long-term design for demolishing me through my very devotion to her needs.

It was carrying the coal buckets that worked the havoc. Sherman always drayed the fuel for both the stove and the fireplace. However, he became quite ill in the dead of winter and was in bed for several weeks. So, of necessity, I took to shoveling the coal. I thought I was quite the Amazon when I lugged my big bucketfuls for the insatiable stove and chopped and carried wood to the equally ravenous fireplace. But I was being subtly undermined.

I had heard of crutch paralysis from time to time throughout my life. In fact, old Mrs. Ferris who first instructed me in the use of crutches had warned me about it when she taught me to protect the brachial nerves by leaning my weight on the palms of my hands, not my armpits. But, frankly, I rather regarded the whole grim idea as an old wives' tale. Even when I began to feel a numbness in my hands, usually noticed in the night or in the morning when I awoke, I assumed that I'd been lying on my arm and that the member had gone to sleep. The fact that shaking my hand quickly brought it to life added evidence to this theory.

When I began to experience a similar sensation during the day, I diagnosed myself as an arthritic and decided to see a doctor on our next trip to Tucson to find out what treatment was prescribed for arthritis. I didn't mention it to Sherman, since he was sick and might get fretful over it. I simply closed my mind to the possibility of crutch paralysis.

My husband wasn't quite as debonair about it when I finally got around to mentioning casually that I had arthritis.

"By the way," I announced one morning when he was up and convalescing waspishly, "I have arthritis now."

"*Arthritis!*" he yelled at me.

"Yes," I said huffily, "arthritis. Can't I have anything? You've been sick for four weeks." I described my symptoms.

"Brachial paralysis!" He kept right on yelling. "Carrying the coal did it." He was sure. "That heavy weight pulling you down hard on the saddles of your crutches." He had me in the car and over ninety miles of rough road to Tucson in an hour and a half.

The doctor confirmed Sherman's diagnosis, not mine. I was, he told me, in the beginning stages of brachial paralysis and I'd have to quit carrying heavy things and leaning all my weight in my armpits while I did it. In fact, I'd have to get off my crutches completely while I did my housework unless I wanted permanently useless arms.

I was determinedly reluctant to accept this medical opinion. I regarded it as a conspiracy between Sherman and the doctor. "If I had come in without crutches," I insisted perversely, "mightn't you have said I had arthritis?" The thought of going back to an artificial leg seemed a dire fate to me.

"Maybe," the doctor said, "but you came in on crutches."

"How do you know you aren't just falling for the obvious?" Sherman dragged me away before I took the name of Hippocrates in vain.

Of course, intellectually, I knew that the doctor had told me the truth and I was merely trying to prove him wrong because I was scared to death. A leg I could get along without nicely, but I was awfully attached to my arms.

Sherman and I made plans to go to California as soon as possible and shop around for a prosthesis.

Curiously coincidental, three days later, an ancient weather-beaten old prospector walked into our yard, leading a burro. It was not at all unusual for a prospector to appear at our house. I'd fed many of them who roamed through our lonely mountain area hunting for pay dirt. They usually could spin wonderful yarns, but none of them ever had a story to tell me comparable in practical worth with this prospector's tale.

He was a brother Elk. "Tim-bah!" Sherman called to me when he saw the old man appear at our gate. He wore a peg leg.

I felt sorry for the old man because I figured he couldn't afford a better prosthesis than a peg. However, he promptly put me right on that score. He felt sorry for me, because I didn't have sense enough to own a peg myself.

"Young lady," he told me solemnly, "you already got yourself a man. If you figger you can keep him without being fancied up all the time, you get yourself a peg. It's a mighty handy thing to have."

He told me about himself. He had been hurt in a mining cave-in, caught under a shattered stull. He had used crutches, of course. You can't escape that phase of development, and he'd also used an artificial leg with all the best modern gadgetry. But by studied choice, he was a devotee of the peg. He traveled over the roughest terrain, climbed mountains, scrambled over rocks, dug shafts, and crawled into them. He rarely knew the luxury of smooth sidewalks.

"The peg is the only prop for a real workingman," he told me.

In his own jargon, he pointed out that the peg is a device that gets down to fundamentals. Any other prosthesis is merely a complication of the basic principle exemplified in the peg—with the addition of articulation and aesthetic qualities. The one-armed man's hook is a similar case in point. It is his basic usable prosthesis, with the artificial hand merely a cosmetic accessory to be worn for inactive dress occasions. The old prospector pointed out that the knee joint and the verisimilitude of shape in the artificial leg add to the appearance of normalcy in the handicapped, but they also add weight and deduct efficiency and security.

He told me that he once went out on a prospecting trip on a fine new artificial leg. He had learned to walk very well—on even floors and paved streets. He was tired, however, before he'd traversed a mile over the rough mountain trails that were an integral part of his normal life. And before he returned (on the burro, with a damaged and useless leg slung on behind the saddlebags), he was fatigued to the point of illness.

"You can't do that to a burro," he explained simply. "Prospecting is all the life I know. I had to do something, so I got me a peg. This one here I got in Tucson. Took the man three days to make it and it cost a quarter of the price of my regular wooden leg from up to Phoenix."

That night Sherman and I decided to go to Tucson in the morning and order a peg to tide me over until such time as we could get someone to take care of our place while we went through the more prolonged custom leg building in California.

The orthopedic fitter who measured me thought I was out of my mind. He kept telling me that he'd never before met a lady who wanted a peg, and his implication that I was certainly no lady was obvious. The whole deal made him frightfully nervous. I think he felt temporarily like a medical quack. He was very anxious to make me an orthodox limb.

"Not just now," I told him. "I'm planning to get a regular artificial leg later, on the Coast."

"You may," he assured me, "put your leg into my hands with confidence."

I had forgotten the solemnity with which most of these craftsmen regard their trade. "There are few gentlemen into whose hands I put my leg with confidence," I said, but I should have held up a sign labeled "Joke: laugh please," because my friend the legmaker wasn't in the mood to cope with a comic. He merely gave me a disturbed grimace and told me with a shudder that I was making a horrible misstep and wasting my fifty dollars.

Actually, I never took a firmer step than that one

nor invested half a hundred more profitably. However, I didn't know it myself at the time. I was inclined to share the orthopedic artisan's dim view.

I felt like a perfect fool when I put the peg on and started using it around the house. There is something basically comical about a Peg Leg Pete—at least, American humor has made it so. However, there was nothing comical in the fact that my paralytic symptoms disappeared almost immediately and I could carry all the coal I wanted to.

In a couple of weeks we went to California and I shopped around and finally ordered myself a $250 leg—a splendid, shapely, glamorous number that I brought back and almost immediately hung in the closet. I put on the peg again.

The old man was quite right. As a workingman's device it couldn't be outsmarted. It was light, and could be put on in the mornings almost as quickly as I could pick up a crutch. It didn't have to be dressed in a stocking and shoe. It played me no temperamental tricks. It was unbending, but as dependable as most virtuous, unbending characters are. It required no repairs and adjustments beyond an occasional new shoulder strap. And, well covered with the leg of my Levis, it scarcely showed. It just gave the rather unusual impression that I was half horse and had a foot on one side and hoof on the other.

There is, I believe, a reason why practically all

French veterans of World War I who lost their legs wore pegs. They preferred them, and in France there were no mild snickers over the device. The wearers were honored for the symbol of their sacrifice. Even Maurice Bunau-Varilla, the owner of *Le Matin* and one of France's wealthiest citizens, always wore a peg leg, and not because he couldn't afford the best and most scientific prosthesis on the market anywhere in the world. He used the peg, one of his acquaintances told me, because it was light, efficient, and completely dependable.

I am still self-conscious about Margaret (Peggy to her intimates). I never venture out of the house on it, except to garden in my own yard. I am just too vain. I put on my artificial leg or, more generally, my crutches, when I face people. Many of my close friends don't even know I possess a peg, since I don't often admit to ownership of this naïve little device. However, if some cold, blizzardy night I were faced with the necessity of chopping up either my artificial leg or my peg for firewood, it would be my fancy, curved confection that would get the ax.

I don't lug coal any more. I now live quite a civilized life, with all the elegant utilities on tap. But I always do my housework on the peg. It is preferable to my highly respected crutches since it leaves my arms free to reach for cobwebs and it allows pliability that the crutches prohibit—bending and stretching. I trust the peg, even if it isn't as cosmetic as a leg, as thoroughly as I would a good precalamity flesh and blood appendage. Moreover, at the end of spring house-cleaning, I may be tired, but it's not from lugging around about twenty pounds of beautifully carved tree.

I don't make a brief for the use of a peg leg by a person who possesses his own knee. These aristocratic unipeds aren't in my class at all. Nor is there any advantage to a man who never leaves the pavement and works at a desk all day. But for anyone with a thigh amputation who has a more active role in life than sitting on a satin sofa and contemplating his own calves, there's nothing like it.

Also, if you're invited to a masquerade and own a peg, you can always dress up like Long John Silver and win first prize. I did, anyway.

CHAPTER XVIII

Gone to the Dogs

IN THE wilderness our social life was not madcap. Week ends we frequently had guests from Tucson—the hardy kind who really liked to rough it and were very useful as woodchoppers. We also occasionally had the "I-love-the-common-people" variety. This species thought we were "just terribly quaint, my dear" and "wasn't it absolutely thrilling getting close to Nature." They were usually useless and invariably got so close to Nature on one visit that they departed with the conviction that it wasn't quaint we were, but crazy.

About once a week we saw our closest friends, Carr and Barbara Tuthill, archaeologists, who were digging up a dead civilization near by. They knew how to cope with our folkways and mores because theirs were similar.

Weekdays when we had any social life, which was rare, it was with our neighbors. This usually consisted of the men in one corner discussing the "feed" (the state of the grass that the cattle grazed on), and the women in another corner "window shopping" together through the Sears Roebuck catalogue.

We did have a temporary dizzy whirl of popularity at the time we put in plumbing. Everyone came to gaze at the wonder of it all. We thought of holding open house with punch ladled from the bathtub. One family, with whom we were only on nodding terms, brought all seven of their children over for an educational call.

These little pets all had running noses that their Mother couldn't catch up with. She was the official custodian of the one family handkerchief, and she swabbed here and there when the situation got really acutely effusive. It was obvious from the beginning that they had all come over merely to try out the new plumbing. Someone was in the bathroom all evening—usually two at a time—one to instruct and one to perform.

One rancher's wife demanded that her husband install plumbing at their place. After all, she argued, if we could have it, why couldn't she?

He gave out with the following incomprehensible logic. "You don't need plumbing," he told her flatly. "They only need it because that poor woman is crippled."

"Honestly!" the ranch wife told me, "it just makes me want to break my leg—I swear it does."

Actually our most congenial and constant companions in the wilderness, of necessity, were animals. A lonely life promotes a strong kinship between animals and humans. This kinship is likely to get completely out of hand, in fact, and become almost pathological. We found ourselves continually comparing our dog's looks and character to that of some our oldest friends and relatives—with the dog winning all the Oscars.

We were on cordial terms with a great variety of creatures. We even had an amiable relationship—or at least a friendly truce—with a skunk who lived under our house. We also had a tame baby bassarisk (the ring-tailed cat) and a tame road runner or paisano, the comical bird of the Southwest who makes better time on foot than on wing.

Our real intimates, however, were Pancho, a huge German shepherd one hundred pounds on the hoof and built on the general lines of a great Dane; and a small runt of a gray tomcat, named "Oscar the Wild," but known to his consorts as "Kitty."

I would gladly have taken a correspondence course in barking and meowing for the privilege of communicating with these two in their own language. The dog, however, was an intellectual. He could understand English. I almost believe he could have spoken it too, if he'd had a mind to. But he was an unpretentious fellow who felt he should remain a dog for appearances' sake. When I got really frantic over silences, I talked to Pancho by the hour. He, more than anyone I ever knew, treated my opinions with grave respect.

Pancho was remarkable. He looked upon most humans with a wary, suspicious eye. We didn't discourage his cynicism. A good ranch watchdog is more valuable than a dozen Yale locks. Nobody ever unlatched our gate, uninvited, when Pancho was on the other side of it announcing his intention to rip the intruder into mouth-size bites. The dog tolerated our friends, but he simply didn't love anyone except Sherman and me—and all other people who used crutches!

He first displayed this gentle quirk in his nature one day when we were in Tucson. Pancho always walked along the city streets on a leash, carrying his aristocratic nose high and peering down it at pedestrians. Frequently people spoke to him admiringly, but he treated them with the disdain of a royal prince grossly insulted by a commoner.

But one day, as we strolled along, his tail started wagging ecstatically and he pulled me right up to a stranger standing by a shop window. The man used crutches. Pancho made a great demonstration of approval. I finally dragged him away.

It didn't occur to me then that it was the crutches that softened the heart of the dog. I merely assumed that from a canine point of view, the stranger, who was none too scrubbed and tidy, must have had a very delicious and meaty smell.

However, when we were in California, Pancho again displayed an instantaneous interest in a crutch user whom we encountered on a tree-inspection tour down San Pasqual Avenue in Pasadena. This was a very neat and fastidious woman. Pancho went right up to her and, showing a great deal of his old-world charm, told her in a most cordial manner that she was a *femme fatale.*

"What a nice, friendly dog," the woman said.

"Well," I explained, "actually, he is generally regarded as a menace to life and limb. You know, I think he likes you because you use crutches."

"All dogs like me," she said, but this was a confession that always left Pancho cold. I was convinced it was the crutches.

Just to test this theory, I took the dog around to call on a two-crutch friend of mine. And instead of snubbing her, which was his usual superior practice with my friends, Pancho greeted her with humble servitude.

•

Anyone on crutches who loves dogs has to watch out for the enthusiastic ones who jump up. A crutch with its basic construction of the split stick, the two parts spread at the top and gradually slanted to join in a ferrule at the bottom, creates a vicious trap for a friendly paw. The first lesson I teach a new puppy is not to jump up—on me, anyway.

In spite of all my communing with animal life, I found time a little heavy on my hands when Sherman was caged up writing Western pulp stories, the cat was off sparring with mice, and the dog was out chasing jack rabbits. I was the only nonprofessional member of the family. To break the habit of tapping my foot against the floor to amuse myself, I also took to writing short stories.

I used the kitchen table as an office desk. To this day, I find that my only touch of artistic temperament is a tendency to work most effectively with the odor of stew or baking beans in the air. When inspiration fails me, I can usually summon it back by cleaning out the refrigerator or baking a pie. I miss the coal bucket, however, on which I used to prop my peg. I have often thought that if I ever get rich and famous I'll buy myself a sterling silver coal scuttle, fill it with hunks of black obsidian, and have it sitting by my desk for a pegstool. I think that would be a rather appropriate whim for an eccentric literary figure.

When I sold my first story I simply couldn't regard the check as serious money. I was too amazed at becoming an "author." The honorarium seemed like a windfall from Heaven, like an inheritance from a distant relative I'd never heard of. I treated it precisely as I used to treat quarters slipped me by an indulgent uncle when I was ten. I went right out and spent it frivolously, buying myself some fancy clothes that I had absolutely no place to wear. Sherman and I still refer to a neat little black number that hung unused for two years in my closet as my "author's dress."

It wasn't until the war and Sherman kissed me farewell and marched off to fight for Old Glory that I began treating my "literary" checks with proper respect—buying bread and bacon and gingham dresses with them.

The war took us away from our little canyon haven. It would have been a perfect place for a draft dodger to hide, as I pointed out to Sherman, but he couldn't get into an enlistment queue fast enough. We packed into our station wagon all our possessions worth transporting, and assigned custody of Chico, the road runner, to the country schoolteacher, who also took over our lease. With the dog and cat, we set off for California. Sherman stowed me away in a cottage at Laguna Beach before rushing off to protect the Four Freedoms.

Pancho, who would have made a splendid hospital orderly in the K-9 Corps, as Comforter First Class to convalescents on crutches, was our only fatal wartime casualty. He was a wilderness dog who recognized the splintered scream of a mountain lion and knew the menace of the dry paperlike crackle of a rattlesnake, but he was naïve about city hazards. One night I let him out for his usual run on the beach before bedtime. I never walked him myself along the shore because crutches sink deep into sand and make hard going. He didn't return.

I called him several times. But since he frequently stayed for long periods, wildly racing the waves along the shore and stirring up the seagulls into white clouds, I wasn't worried until a young man came and knocked on my door.

"Is your dog here?" he asked me. Somehow I could tell that this was only a rhetorical question.

"No," I answered. "No, he isn't here." I suddenly had a stomach full of sick fear.

"I'm afraid your dog is badly hurt," the young man told me. "He tried to get home but he fell just down the street. It must have been a hit and run driver on the blacked out highway. I recognized him as the big black dog who belonged to the girl on crutches, so I started hunting for you, even though I didn't know your name. A man three doors down said that a girl on crutches lived in this house. A friend of mine is getting his car. We'll drive you to the veterinarian."

"You're very kind," I said, "but I have a car."

"No, it would be best if we drove you through the dimout. It's probably hard for you to drive."

Tenderly these two good Samaritans lifted the broken body of the beautiful dog into their car. With gasoline more precious than Chanel No. 5, they drove me eight miles along the war-darkened coast highway to a veterinarian.

The dog knew, I think, that his head rested in my lap. He gave a deep, shuddering sigh, half agony and half content, before he died. If it hadn't been for my identifying crutches, my dear old friend would have had to depart in loneliness. It is curious what strange purposes they have served.

Sherman bought me a frisky, leaky, new German shepherd puppy on his next leave. He was an engaging little fellow and I loved him, but he never quite filled my heart, which was stretched to accommodate the big, crutch-loving old Pancho.

I wish I had done as much for the war effort as my crutches did for me during the war. In a patriotic effort to keep Democracy alive, I finally had to wear my artificial leg when I went to stand in a meat line. Frenzied women, frantic for a smell of beef, would still push me and my crutches right up to a counter ahead of themselves. I always felt so apologetic that I'd have only enough courage to ask for a soup bone. Since I figured I'd probably get rickets before the war was over on such rations, I wore the leg. On it, I was allowed to take my turn and fight honorably for my half-pound of hamburger.

One friendly butcher didn't allow himself to be fooled by my democratic little disguise, however. "Got to fill up that hollow leg," he whispered like a conspirator, and howled over his high wit while he swayed and banged his hand against his bloody apron. "I saved you a roast."

There is a point beyond which nobility of nature simply can't beat down temptation. I ate disgustingly well during the war.

Sherman was in the Army only a scant year. They decided he wasn't quite durable enough for their purposes. They gave him an honorable discharge to bring home, along with his chronic sinusitus. But durable or not durable, he got back just in time to engage in a more strenuous bout than basic training. Our beach cottage was sold over our heads and we went forth to bat out our brains against the housing shortage.

CHAPTER XIX

The Face on the Cuttingroom Floor

During our frantic house-hunting pilgrimage, whenever we could outmaneuver them, we moved in on our relatives. Our most tolerant hosts were Sherman's parents, who welcomed us with convincing enthusiasm at their home in Pasadena. They even put up a good front of stoic calm when their cook departed with a couple of unkind cuts at how much we ate. She also mentioned an aversion for our dog and made it clear that our cat's habit of bringing his mice to the kitchen door to show off before consuming them was ill bred and upsetting to a refined, high-minded kitchen queen.

It was in Pasadena that Sherman had a sinus operation and I had a movie offer. We both nearly died of our respective shocks.

I was walking along Colorado Boulevard in Pasadena one day when a puffy little citizen raced up behind me. "Wait! You with the crutches. Just a minute," he yelled. I waited.

"Say, young lady," he panted, "would you like a job with the movies?"

"What have you got to offer?" I asked in a feeble attempt at the grand manner.

"I haven't anything myself, but get hold of today's paper. I saw an ad in there. You fill the bill exactly. I've got to run—catch my bus."

With that, he was gone. Of course, I grabbed every paper on the newsstand. It was there, all right. "WANTED: a girl with an amputated leg for movie work. Would prefer one who uses crutches habitually. Good pay and easy work."

The two latter lures always appeal to me, even when they aren't tied up with the movies. The combination was irresistible.

"How would this do for an opener in my application letter?" I said to Sherman that night. "My friends all say I am fascinating. Why, just today I was walking along when someone called me Ann Sheridan—open-and-shut case of mistaken identity."

"Surprise them," Sherman advised cynically. "Let Mr. Goldwyn say, 'Why, Miss Sheridan, don't tell me you hacked off your leg just for this little old part?' "

"I wonder what studio it is," I day-dreamed like an adolescent. "I bet it's Twentieth Century-Fox. They're casting for the *Song of Bernadette*. Jennifer Jones is probably even now planning to grow me a new leg for a minor miracle."

I finally wrote a dignified little note swimming over what a charmer I was. I merely admitted to my fulfillment of the amputation requirement. I sent it off to the anonymous box number given in the ad.

The next day I had a telephone call. It was the movie magnate. He told me his name, but it didn't sound familiar. He wasn't Louis B. Mayer, anyway, or Darryl Zanuck. He asked me a few questions. The only one I can remember was, "How old are you?"

I crossed my fingers and said twenty-five. If he questioned that later, I figured I could always tell him I had lived recklessly and was considerably jaded for my years. He made an appointment to call on me.

He arrived the next day with some henchman in tow. "Look, she even wears the white crutches," one of the men said the first thing when they came into the house.

"Yes, very interesting, very interesting indeed—"

This, I gathered, was dandy. I must say I was startled when I discovered why. They were casting the lead, they told me, for a Government-sponsored film for distribution to servicemen and foreign audiences, on the life of the famous one-legged French prostitute who habitually used white crutches. Her part in the underground resistance movement was a courageous and fascinating story and would prove a great morale builder when depicted on the screen.

"She has now disappeared from Paris and no one

knows what happened to her, whether she was spirited away by friends or whether her role was discovered by the Nazis. I don't suppose you have heard of her?" the casting one asked.

"Well, *rather!*" I said. It was difficult to forget my encounter on the Place de l'Opera with the sad-eyed young man who had advised me passionately to throw away my white crutches.

Before they departed, they informed me that they were completely satisfied. The part was mine. I would hear from them shortly when the picture was ready to go into production. I asked the leader of the intrigue for his name and studio connection. He scrawled them out on a piece of paper.

That night I decided it might be just as well to find out a little about my producer before I signed up as a prostitute with him. I called up everyone I knew who hobnobbed with the higher brackets in Hollywood. Nobody had ever heard of my man. I even called everyone I knew who had so much as eaten a square meal at the Brown Derby, but I drew a blank.

Finally I tracked down an acquaintance who was as ignorant as all the rest about the mysterious stranger, but he, as casting director of a large studio, was in a position to make effective inquiry.

He telephoned "my" studio. "My" man was not known. That was deflating. An Army moving-picture unit occupying a corner of the lot didn't know him either. The O.W.I. office in Los Angeles in charge of government wartime films, never heard of him, nor were they scheduling the story described. They were, in fact, closing their offices that very day. The studio legal department got somewhat fretful and excited. But if it was a racket, it certainly was a peculiarly subtle one, with a very specialized species of victims.

I hated to give up my movie man. "Maybe he was somebody terribly important, slumming under a false namc," I told Sherman. "You know, out getting close to the common people."

"Yes," said Sherman. "He was probably Pandro S. Berman, out 'Pandroing' incognito."

From that day to this I have heard nothing more from my movie magnates. They came, they looked me over, told me I was a great find, and left. What they were up to is anyone's guess. I for one have contrived some magnificent plots.

If they wanted to locate a certain, particular one-legged girl by putting out the irresistible bait of a movie job, they probably found her. I wouldn't know. But obviously, they weren't looking for me. I'm still my old undiscovered self.

But if I never "made Hollywood" as an actress I did sell a book to the movies. It was titled *Party Line* and related a few odds and ends of juicy gossip that I picked up during a misspent youth listening in on the telephone. For the most part, it was written in Prescott, Arizona, where the waves of the housing problem finally washed us ashore. Here not only desperation but delight in the place and the people turned us into immovable landmarks. We quit trying to rent a housc and bought one, a small cottage formerly owned and occupied by a nice old lady.

Instead of throwing it out, which might have been the wiser course, she threw in her furniture along with the house. Artistically speaking, the most dominant piece we acquired thus was probably the stiff, carved Victorian settee in the living room, or possibly the picture which hung over it of a flimsily draped female sitting by a waterfall bathing her clean, bare feet.

From my own personal point of view, however, nothing pierced my emotions quite so sharply as the black coal stove in the kitchen. The house was only three years old and was well plumbed and equipped with other modern devices. But the old lady apparently had one psychopathic quirk. She would have no truck with newfangled stoves.

It had been my equally firm intention never to have any more truck with the old-fashioned, black-sided, blackhearted ones. However, we knew this was Custer's last stand. Our despair was such that we would have happily accepted a wigwam with central heating—a bonfire in the middle. We'd even have taken six Hopi boarders, if they came with the place.

So, my book was composed on a kitchen table, with my peg again propped up comfortably on a coal scuttle. This may have been a tonic for my artistic temperament, but it was an irritant to my human temper. Civilization had weakened me.

As winter advanced and the snow heaped up around the coal cellar and Sherman collapsed with sinusitus, the rationing board took pity on me. They gave me a certificate for a new gas range. "That poor woman . . ." "Sad case . . ." ". . . one-legged, you know . . ."

How firm a foundation! Praise the Lord!

My reputation for being not only physically crippled but something of a lame brain probably prompted the question that one local citizen put to my husband when my book was published. "Say, would you mind my inquiring how much it cost you?"

"What do you mean?" Sherman asked.

"Did the printing run high? My wife's written a lot of junk, too—poems and such like—and she'd like to get it published, and I just wondered how much that sort of thing sets you back. You don't figure to cover your expenses on the book sales, do you? Nobody's got that many kinfolks." He chortled merrily. "Of course, with you it's different," he went on seriously. "You'll get rid of a lot of copies to people who'll buy it because your wife's crippled."

I am glad, for the health of my royalties, that the book sold in a few places besides my own home town. But it wasn't my name on a national best-seller list that warmed my heart and made me feel important. It was the string of customers who bought out the local supply of my book in half an hour after it went on the block. With these purchasers, buying the book wasn't an impersonal transaction. In most cases, they didn't know whether the critics said it was tripe or a treasure. They bought the book because I wrote it and they wanted to see me get ahead in the world.

What is an anonymous customer compared to the eager little boy who stood in line, representing his widowed mother who worked and couldn't get time off to come for her copy? He had his two dollars and fifty cents clutched in his fist and he whispered to me as I autographed his book.

"We already got seven books," he said proudly, "but Mama decided to buy your book anyway—you being crippled and she knows you, besides. Loraine gets to read it first because she washed dishes all week. Mama's going to read it nights when us kids are in bed. Fred's going to read it second, and Jane's going to read it out loud to me third. Then Mama's going to send it to Grandma to read and then we're going to keep it on the table right between Papa's picture and the goldfish."

Another customer, a sweet old lady, patted me on the shoulder while I inscribed her copy. "We're all proud of you, dear," she said. "As I said to my daughter, something worth while came out of your misfortune. If you hadn't had to sit down and rest so often, I expect you'd never have had the time to write a book, would you? I guess you'd be the first to admit that some good resulted from your being handicapped."

For that latter bit of philosophy anyway, there is no argument. I certainly would be the first to admit that quite a bit of good has come from my being handicapped. For one thing, I can't possibly imagine what in Heaven's name there would have been to put in this, my autobiography, if I'd had two feet.

THE END